The years fly by....
but the days last
Forever!

A Biblical Guide to Urgent and Intentional Parenting

CATHY DURRENBERG

The years fly by....
but the days last
Forever!

A Biblical Guide to Urgent and Intentional Parenting

CATHY DURRENBERG

WESTBOW·
PRESS
A DIVISION OF THOMAS NELSON
& ZONDERVAN

Scripture quotations are from The Holy Bible, English Standard Version®
(ESV®), copyright © 2001 by Crossway, a publishing ministry of
Good News Publishers. Used by permission. All rights reserved.

WestBow Press books may be ordered through booksellers or by contacting:

WestBow Press
A Division of Thomas Nelson & Zondervan
1663 Liberty Drive
Bloomington, IN 47403
www.westbowpress.com
1 (866) 928-1240

Because of the dynamic nature of the Internet, any web addresses or
links contained in this book may have changed since publication and
may no longer be valid. The views expressed in this work are solely those
of the author and do not necessarily reflect the views of the publisher,
and the publisher hereby disclaims any responsibility for them.

Any people depicted in stock imagery provided by Thinkstock are
models, and such images are being used for illustrative purposes only.
Certain stock imagery © Thinkstock.

ISBN: 978-1-4908-4282-0 (sc)
ISBN: 978-1-4908-4303-2 (e)

Library of Congress Control Number: 2014911527

Printed in the United States of America.

WestBow Press rev. date: 7/11/2014

Contents

Preface ix

Acknowledgments..xiii

1   In the Beginning 1

2   Practical Goals of Parenting..3

3   Who Are You? 9

4   Parenting Styles 14

5   Discipline, Discipline, Discipline!....................................28

6   Being *the* Role Model to Your Children..........................45

7   Communication Required 66

8   Spiritual Disciplines and Emerging Faith 81

9   No Greater Love 93

10 A Very Brief History of Family Life
    throughout the Ages..97

Sources..113

To my supportive husband, Jon, who is always willing to hear me out. Thank you for putting God first in all things!

To Abby, Liz, and Andy, who are the three greatest blessings two people could ask for!

Preface

I believe there is a new a wave of thinking that is emerging in the "church" world. The David Platts, Francis Chans, Rob Turners, Chuck Davises, and others like them in the United States are making a strong statement for the church to return to its roots that are founded in the Bible. For too long we have been caught up in the denominational traditions and rituals of the faith, and the Jesus of the Bible has been lost. Many areas of parenting have been turned upside down too, and parents need to return to the Bible for guidance and direction for the future of their children.

I have lived one of those Christian stories that go like this: I grew up in the church, but I never really lived out its teachings in my life. The church I was raised in was pretty typical, with Sunday services, a few Bible studies, youth groups, and a choir. As a kid, I wasn't excited about going, but I didn't fight it either. Really, it was no big deal one way or another.

Later, after many years of pursuing bad decisions during college and my early twenties, I married my high school sweetheart, Jon, and we had three beautiful children. We knew that raising our kids in the church was important, but there was still not much substance behind our actions or faith. We attended the church I grew up in, falling back into the same old routine, until …

Ruth Senter was speaking at a women's conference in Cincinnati, and I was invited to attend. She spoke the truth about needing God in our lives and the importance of raising our children to follow Him. It was as if I was the only one in the room, and God met me there. The Holy Spirit took hold of my heart that weekend, and I have never been the same. What followed was a yearning to know God better and a desire to live more like Jesus.

Well, God immediately put me to work. I was asked to establish and run a preschool at our church, and three months later I found myself on staff, leading the preschool, nursery, and childcare departments. Jon and I both believed that it was important to be home for our kids when they were not yet in school, but our youngest was now in the first grade, and suddenly I found myself working full time. I enjoyed it, but life got extra busy, and Jesus sort of took a back seat for a time. It is remarkable how we can get so involved doing church work that we lose sight of the work of the church, and that is what happened to me.

Thankfully, God has been extremely patient with me over the years. One day I was walking to my car after work, and I very clearly felt God reminding me that He was my priority and that I needed to spend more time with Him. I didn't feel as though I had strayed that far, but in reality I was manipulating Him in and out of my life in order to maintain a schedule rather than making Him my all in all. God deserves more than to merely fit into a compartment of our lives!

So, how did this whole book idea come to fruition? Well, in 2005, as a newly appointed pastor, I decided to go back to school and get my master's degree. The Alliance Theological Seminary had a branch campus nearby, and I joined the cohort that met every Thursday for two and a half years. The focus of our degree was Christian ministry with an emphasis in leadership, and God continually placed young parents on my heart. Before the end of year one, I knew I would write my thesis on parents becoming the leaders of their homes.

God pointed me to leadership concepts that were effective in the business world but also valid in the home. Developing respect and productive communication and setting goals were a few of the areas identified as necessary components for companies and parents alike. Slowly the paper took shape, but more noticeably, my heart's desire to impact families grew and grew.

Throughout those two and a half years, my views on the church as an institution and on the way we led the parents changed greatly as I gained more knowledge of the Bible and basic leadership principles. I believed that the parents needed to be empowered and taught how to be the spiritual leaders in their homes—and that the church should be assisting and supporting this effort, not leading it. In 2006 it was time for me to move on, and I resigned from my pastoral position. Once again, God had a new direction for my life.

I graduated in June 2007 with a master's degree in Professional Studies, and I am happy to report that my thesis, *Training and Equipping the Parents to be the Spiritual Leaders of Their Homes*, got an A! The hard work was well worth it, and I am blessed to have had that educational experience. My advisor mentioned a few times that I should write a book on parenting, but it took me seven years to take those comments seriously. For the past six years, I have worked as a paraprofessional with multihandicapped students, and God has said that now is the time.

So here it is. When God tells you to do something, you just do it! I appreciate this quote by Tom Kizziar: "Our greatest fear as individuals and as a church should not be of failure but of succeeding at things in life that don't matter." It is my prayer that parents everywhere will understand that raising their children is their number one priority. Parents are their children's primary resource and connection to Jesus Christ, and unless children see Christ living through their parents, kids may miss that connection. It's hard work every day, but we cannot sit back and let the world determine whom their children will follow. Let's focus daily on what truly matters!

"You are the light of the world. A city set on a hill cannot be hidden" (Matthew 5:14 ESV).

Acknowledgments

Thank you to my dear friends Ruth Sapp and Sue Kelzer for proofing some of my work. Your input was greatly appreciated!

Thanks also to Stephen Julian for your encouragement and wisdom over the years!

1

In the Beginning

"The years fly by, but the days last forever!" The unknown author of this quote spoke a truth that still resonates with me today. My children have grown, but in the days when they were ages four, three, and one, I was too tired and overwhelmed to truly give those words much thought. I woke up at unthinkable hours, attempted to shop for groceries, provided healthy meals, dealt with spats and squabbles, considered preschool options, gave needed attention to each child, and did countless other things before the dreaded, nightly task of getting ready for bed. Phew! This routine continued for several years, and I selfishly wondered if it would ever end.

Years passed, and the events of the days changed. We experienced our son's first baseball games in which the kids pitched for the first time. This seemed to be a pivotal year, when little boys often decided either to continue baseball or call it quits. Watching the batters get clunked time and time again was painful. We also attended swim meets—where our daughter was in the third and the seventy-eighth events—and dance recitals that seemed to never end. But now all of these things are over for us.

Then we moved into the teen years. Oh, the teen years! We waited for the end of school to hear how a big exam went. We taught all three kids to drive, and then we sat in the license bureau, waiting for them to return from the driving test. We dealt with the pain of a breakup, and we sat and waited anxiously at ten minutes past curfew. Now these things are completely in our past. Time has truly flown by, and *now* we fully understand the wisdom and truth of that saying.

Throughout your child's life, you, the parent, will be the most influential person to him or her. My husband, Jon, and I are now "empty nesters," and we still see the important role that we play as parents to our grown children. Parenting no longer involves the day-to-day endeavors, but being a parent never ends—only the manner in which we relate to our children.

Remember that all children are gifts from God. Even though some days may seem endless, our time with our children is short. Children are innocent and pliable, and they deserve to be taken care of. The world will be vying for your children's attention, but you must be the ones who directs their steps and leads them down the path to adulthood.

2

Practical Goals of Parenting

When our three children were young, Jon and I set goals for parenting that we believed would equip them for adulthood. We thought it was important to encourage and support them in any way we could, emotionally, socially, educationally, spiritually, and physically.

Each child had a different temperament and personality, so we tried to be flexible in how we disciplined them. Being the best role models for them and showing them Jesus through our words and actions was very important to us, but some days went better than others. We were not afraid to apologize, though the fact is, we could have done it more often. In a nutshell, Jon and I did the best we could.

I think it is important for you to meet the cast of characters— my children—before we get started. I will refer to them throughout the book. Maybe you will find some character traits in them that align with your own children. Each is very different, but thankfully, they have all made Jesus the Lord of their lives, and no parent could hope for more.

Our oldest, Abby, is on staff with YWAM (Youth with a Mission) in Tyler, Texas. She trains and equips students to know

God and to know who they are in Christ. Many, like her, become missionaries to all corners of the world after attending this training. As a child, Abby was unafraid of anyone and seemed to get along better with boys than with other girls. She took on the worries and concerns of all of her friends and tried to help them. While she has never had one best friend, Abby has had—and still has—hundreds of friends. She is one of the kindest and friendliest people I know. Next June, Abby will be getting married to a godly man, Robby, in a "Texas" style wedding!

Our daughter Liz is thirteen months younger than Abby. She currently lives in Los Angeles, where she is a recent graduate of the American Music and Dramatic Academy. Liz aspires to become an actress, dancer, and singer. She had an impressive vocabulary when she was younger and was cautious and wary of those around her. She usually enjoyed having one or two special friends. Today, her mission field looks quite different from Abby's, but I think many would agree that a godly presence in Hollywood and the entertainment world is quite pressing. She will be getting married to a wonderful guy named Andrew this summer.

Andy is our third child and only son. He is a student at the University of Cincinnati, where he studies criminal justice. This career path is ideal for him. His strong-willed nature lends itself to fighting for what he believes is right. He has been to Malawi, Africa, and Cap Haitian, Haiti, to serve children in orphanages. He truly has a servant's heart. After graduation, we would not be one bit surprised if Andy headed into the mission field overseas. Many stories in this book are experiences we had with him over the years. Strong-willed kids make life very interesting!

Let's start our discussion with the goals that we would like to achieve for our kids as we lead them into adulthood.

Unfortunately, there are two sets of potential goals. The world has one set of goals for them, but thankfully, God has a different and better version for our families.

The World's Goals

The world tells us that a successful life means being well-educated, happy, and self-sufficient, having a fulfilling career, finding deep meaning and significance within ourselves, providing every need or desire for our families, raising healthy, obedient children, living life to the fullest, and then retiring so we can enjoy the rest of our lives living on the hard-earned money we made in the work force. Does this sound pretty close?

Many of these ideas arise from a never-ending array of worldly ideas and thoughts on parenting.

Psychology classes across America discuss J. B. Watson, who wrote a book in 1930 called *Behaviorism*. Its premise was that a child can be conditioned at an early age and, through behavior modifications, can grow to live a successful life.

Dr. Spock of the 1980s said that we are to listen to our kids' feelings and be their friends. This embraced the notion that participation is the key to success and that we are all winners.

Gloria Steinem empowered women to take charge of their own lives and work in a "man's world."

Ellen DeGeneres believes one thing, and Dr. Phil purports another.

Parenting magazine and *Psychology Today* offer advice and opinions on all sorts of parental topics.

None of these influences in themselves have changed families, but they are a few that have spoken to the way we raise our kids and live our lives.

God's Goals

Now, here is what I believe are God's long-term goals for us: to love Him and to love others, which is the Great Commandment. This seems simple enough, but what does that look like as we lead our children? Well, I believe it should look something like this: nurturing a deep and abiding relationship with Jesus Christ, modeling and promoting a genuine love for others, preparing and supporting our children for whatever God has called them to do, and equipping them to persevere when hardships occur.

In his book, *Don't Waste Your Life*, John Piper states that our goal for life is this: "Whatever you do, find the God centered, Christ exalting, Bible saturated passion of your life, and find your way to say it and live for it and die for it. Make a difference this way!" I agree.

Clearly the world has its own ideals for the future, yet real success is found when we accept the life God has for us, when we become, by His grace, what He has called us to be. Here are some benefits of following His ways:

- Significance will grow when we focus on positive activities that are eternal.
- Fulfillment is found when we fully understand our identities in Christ and we use the gifts and talents that He has given us to edify others and to glorify the Lord.

- Satisfaction comes from living righteously and continually trying to improve relationships and service to others, which leads to a greater purpose for our lives.
- Peace is internal. When we control our thoughts and emotions, God's peace reigns in our lives.
- Happiness is wanting what we have.
- Fun is unrestrained and spontaneous. We remove unscriptural influences and become free.
- Security is found in Christ alone!

Each day, we all must decide whom we will follow—the world or Jesus. This reality then speaks into our daily lives and shapes and molds our actions and thoughts. Sometimes we cannot decide, so we dangle our legs over the fence into both camps. Thoughts like "I want to do the right thing, but it's hard!" or "I've always been a good person" or even "God doesn't really care about that!" stream through our thinking. At the end of the day, we feel "okay" about ourselves, and God was free to join us whenever He wanted to jump in.

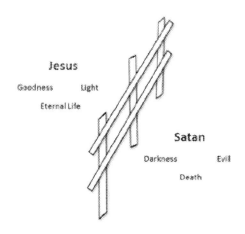

We find Satan on one side of the fence and Jesus on the other side. But here's the catch: Satan owns the fence. If we only live for God *sometimes* and have not put our full trust in Him, then, sadly, we are not for Him. Walking by faith is simply choosing to believe what God says is true and living accordingly by the power of the Holy Spirit. Understanding who we are in Him is foundational to anything and everything we do.

So what does that mean for us? Read on.

3

Who Are You?

If I were to ask you who you are, what would your response be? I could say that I am Cathy Durrenberg. I am a US citizen. I am a mom, wife, sister, daughter, and aunt. I am five foot six inches tall, and I have brown hair and brown eyes. All of these are true by worldly standards, but none get to the heart of who I really am.

I am a child of the one, true King of the universe!

Did you know that in order to *live* like a child of God, you first must *believe* and *understand* that you are a child of God? We are accepted, secure, and significant! Nothing or no one can change this truth, and nothing will supersede its importance. If we really understood this, I wonder if our lives would be lived out differently? The fact is that we find ourselves at odds with the world.

The word *divergent* is in vogue these days. This may be due, in part, to the book series by that name or to the recent release of a movie trilogy. I would like to relate the concept to a new generation of followers of Jesus Christ who are choosing to be divergent and are refusing to be like this world. Our standards for living are in the Bible, and we no longer live for this safe, comfy existence we are accustomed to. If Jesus has rescued you from this world, I want to challenge you to stand out and live like there's no tomorrow!

Romans 12:2 tells us, "Do not be conformed to this world, but be transformed by the renewal of your mind, that by testing you may discern what is the will of God, what is good and acceptable and perfect." This process of spiritual transformation would be nearly impossible except for the fact that you are a child of God!

Who we are in Christ is foundational to how we live our lives. When we accept Jesus as our Lord and Savior, we become children of God. All of the following statements are true, and you cannot do anything to make them more true. You can, however, make these traits more meaningful and productive in your life by simply opting to believe what God has said about you in His Word. It is not prideful to accept these truths for yourself, but it may be defeating if you don't! (The italicized words are my own emphasis.)

- I am a child of God. "But to all who did receive him, who believed in his name, he gave the right to become *children of God*" (John 1:12).
- I am the light of the world. "You are the *light of the world*" (Matthew 5:14).
- I am Christ's friend. "No longer do I call you servants, for the servant does not know what his master is doing; but I have called you *friends*" (John 15:15).
- I am a joint heir with Christ, sharing his inheritance. "And if children, then heirs—heirs of God and fellow heirs with Christ," (Romans 8:17), "a joint heir with Christ sharing His inheritance with Him" (John 15:15a).

- I am a member of Christ's body. "Now you are the *body of Christ* and individually members of it" (1 Corinthians 12:27).
- I am a new creation. "Therefore, if anyone is in Christ, he is a *new creation*. The old has passed away; behold, the new has come" (2 Corinthians 5:17).
- I am a saint. "To the church of God that is in Corinth, to those sanctified in Christ Jesus, called to be *saints* together with all those who in every place call upon the name of our Lord Jesus Christ, both their Lord and ours" (1 Corinthians 1:2). "Paul, an apostle of Christ Jesus by the will of God, to the *saints* who are in Ephesus, and are faithful in Christ Jesus" (Ephesians 1:1).
- I am a citizen of heaven, seated in heaven right now. "But our *citizenship is in heaven*, and from it we await a Savior, the Lord Jesus Christ" (Ephesians 2:6). "And raised us up with him and *seated us with him in the heavenly places* in Christ Jesus" (Philippians 3:20).
- I am chosen of God, holy and dearly loved. "Put on then, as God's *chosen ones, holy and beloved,* compassionate hearts, kindness, humility, meekness, and patience" (Colossians 3:12). "For we know, brothers loved by God, that he has *chosen* you" (1 Thessalonians 1:4).
- I am an enemy of the Devil. "Be sober-minded; be watchful. *Your adversary the devil* prowls around like a roaring lion, seeking someone to devour" (1 Peter 5:8).

The only formula that is meaningful in God's kingdom is this: you + Christ = new significance for life as a child of God. It is not what you do as a Christian that determines who you are; it is who you are that determines what you do.

Our son, Andy, played high school football for a very successful program. It was a year-round endeavor, and guys who played more than one sport usually had to decide to narrow that down to one, especially if one was football. At times we all got very competitive and wrapped up in the team's success—most definitely to an unhealthy degree.

Day in and day out, football consumed our lives. Andy spent numerous hours practicing or in the weight room, I was in the football mothers' club, and Jon was in the quarterback club. Our identities were skewed, big time! One day as I was watching a practice, God spoke to me in a powerful way. I was utterly convicted that my life—and my family's life—was way too obsessed with a sport, and God had been lost in the busyness. At that moment, I prayed for forgiveness and asked God to keep us from ever again losing our identities in Christ to football or any other distraction.

Satan constantly schemes to distort who we are. He can't change God, and he can't do anything to change our identities and positions in Christ. If we believe Satan's lies, we will live as though our identities in Christ aren't true. So when you see yourself as a child of God who is spiritually alive in Christ, you will begin to live accordingly. If you're like me, you begin to have a whole new confidence in the many roles you fill, especially that of parent.

Please don't ever forget that we do nothing to become special or chosen. It's all God's doing. His grace makes us who we are. All we did was respond to His invitation, and since that time, we have every right to enjoy our special relationship with our heavenly Father. Knowledge of who you are is absolutely the most important truth you and your children can possess.

"See what kind of love the Father has given to us that we should be called children of God; and so we are. The reason why the world does not know us is that it did not know him. Beloved, we are God's children now, and what we will be has not yet appeared; but we know that when he appears we shall be like him, because we shall see him as he is" (1 John 3:1–2).

4

Parenting Styles

Jon and I were raised in the same town of Kettering, Ohio, attended the same high school, graduated the same year, went to college, and then were married at the age of twenty-seven. Much of our early lives was similar, but we entered the world of parenting with different ideals. While my parents were more on the permissive side, his were quite strict, so it became necessary—first in marriage and then in parenthood—to find a balance and to work together to establish our own style. The way we had been raised, along with what we identified as effective parenting skills, played major factors in our decisions.

There are a number of various parenting styles, but I will present four primary ones. I believe it is important to understand your current or perceived parenting style, even though you may fit into more than one category, which is okay. This is not an indictment of one style or another, but there is one that stands out as the most promising and healthiest for our children.

Style 1: Permissive and Full of Love

This first style of parenting exhibits few demands, and these parents try not to upset the child. They are very responsive to their children but are not demanding. They are full of love for their children, and the need to discipline is not a priority. The term *super love* is applied to these families because they often feel that telling their children what to do is not necessary. They believe that children will figure life out on their own when they get older, and that their actions, good or bad, are to be expected at a certain age. The "terrible twos" will simply be terrible. Teens will be defiant and sassy because that is what teens do.

With this parenting style, it is not uncommon for children to get almost everything they want without working for it. A child's demand for expensive items is carefully generated through millions of dollars spent on advertising by manufacturers. The trouble is that the parents often *can* afford to buy a new item—if not with cash, at least with a handy credit card. Some children get the desired items when Mom and Dad feel pressured, sometimes by guilt, to buy those things. In this vein, it has been said that "prosperity and success offer a greater test of character than does adversity." I agree.

Parents who overindulge their children with the "things" they crave interfere with a true sense of appreciation. The saturation principle says that you "cheat a child of pleasure" when you give him everything he wants. True happiness is not in having what you want but in wanting what you have! How unfortunate that a child may never have the chance to long for something, to dream about it and plot for it each day. If allowed to do so, he may even get desperate enough to work for it!

Finally, because lenient parents do not provide clear boundaries through discipline, they create insecurities. These parents love their child dearly, but because they are unsure of limits, the child pushes them, wondering when will they say no. Impulsiveness and misconduct can be common because the child has not learned to control his behavior. He may always expect to get his way and will struggle to accept circumstances.

Down the road, these children may exhibit a greater risk of heavy drinking during the teenage years. They continue to push and disobey because they want someone to say no. Kids do not wake up each day and think about how they can rebel or be difficult. Often they act out because they don't understand that what they are doing is not acceptable—because no one has taught them.

A friend and I were at Panera one Saturday morning when I heard a whistle sound. I'm not sure if my friend Ruth noticed it, but every few seconds the whistle blew, and a woman responded, "Stop it!" This repeated five or six more times. Generally, there is a low murmur of chatting in this place, but people were beginning to look around to find the source of the irritant.

Eventually I noticed a young mom (with someone who may have been her mother) trying to control a three-year-old boy, who was not happy to be trapped in the booth next to her. When their food came, all was quiet for a short time—until approximately ten minutes later when the whistle sounded again.

The next thing I knew, the little guy was standing on the floor, and I could see that the annoying whistle was attached to a lanyard with keys on it around his neck. He danced around and blew the whistle a couple more times, and the adults around him became noticeably bothered by his actions. The boy was oblivious to the disrespect he was showing to those around him, and he seemed to enjoy the attention he was receiving.

I, of course, was more exasperated by the lack of proper correction coming from the mom. She appeared to be at a loss as to how to curb her son's antics, and she basically did nothing. Simply taking away the lanyard would have been a first step in helping the situation, but this did not happen. I am fairly certain that she felt the boy would have thrown a fit and caused a scene if she did—as if this wasn't already the case. Discipline, in this case, was greatly missing, and unless that mom gets a grip on her son soon, his behavior will only deteriorate.

This indulgent, undisciplined manner of parenting has me particularly concerned. Maybe you are a product of this parenting style. Or perhaps you are a permissive parent. If so, I want to say this to you in love. Permissive parenting is not effective, and here's why: the kids' self-esteem may be high, but they focus too much on themselves. The feelings of such children are protected to the point that they rarely have to deal with uncomfortable situations.

For example, we have become so concerned about our children neither winning nor losing in sports that we eliminate all competition and create participation awards. As parents, we sign kids up for an activity or sport, perhaps pay for it, drive them there, rearrange our schedules to watch events, attend a banquet— and then *they* get a participation award! Our kids should be grateful to us for allowing them to do the activity, but we put all the focus on them, and then we lose the opportunity for many teachable moments!

In the past, if a child was in trouble at school, he could expect double trouble at home. Nowadays, parents are marching up to the principal's office and blaming everyone (except their children) for the problems that are occurring!

At the high school where I work, a student athlete was caught stealing food from the cafeteria more than once. His parents did not like that he was suspended from school for two days, which meant that he could not wrestle in the district tournament that night. They called the superintendent of the schools, and somehow the local news media became involved. To make a long story short, the boy's parents created a frenzy over a wrestling meet, and their sixteen-year-old son received the message that the consequences for stealing should be nullified if you are a good athlete. Do you believe the parents were doing the right thing?

Our children should feel empowered, but that does not translate to entitlement. The feeling or belief that you deserve something merely because you are alive is the crux of entitlement. Upon adulthood, these children struggle in the work force, and their work ethic is diminished. They expect to be coddled, and they don't adjust well to the structure and expectations of the work culture. I'll address this issue further at the end of this chapter.

While your children are still in your home, it is your choice to be lenient or permissive with them. But be prepared if others see your children as spoiled rotten or bratty. Many of these children are self-centered, rude, and demanding. Often the parents are the one's who complain about this, but they fail to look inward to see how their children got that way!

It's understandable that we want our children to be happy, but many kids equate "things" and outside activities with happiness. Eventually they will have to work hard and get along with other adults. Our Western culture suffers when we saturate children with materialism. If this is how you parent, please consider the ramifications.

Style 2: Authoritative and In Charge

Next, we'll take a look at the authoritative parent. These parents are quite demanding and are not as responsive to their child's opinions or thoughts as other parents may be. Obedience is the number-one priority, and these parents have high expectations that the children will conform and comply with the parent's rules and guidelines. Often raised by a strong, forceful parent themselves, these leaders feel that they must exert their authority in order to show the child who is in charge.

Authoritative parents—or sometimes just one of the parents (usually Dad)—are primarily strict disciplinarians, and they expect respect for their work and efforts. They show love by taking care of the child's needs and providing the items they deem necessary. Spending time together and having nice chats and appropriate physical affection can be missing with this manner of parenting. Dialogue between the child and parent might be lacking because these parents do not feel the need to explain the reasoning behind their rules and boundaries. "Do it because I said so!" is a familiar response.

Children from this type of parenting situation may struggle with creativity and initiative, as their parents have not supported them or encouraged them to think for themselves. Social skills may also be lacking because when the rules are laid down, they are not given choices but are told how to think. This can lead to insecurities, self-esteem issues, rebellion, and much discord. Eventually a child will count down the days until he can leave the house.

When love is missing, children view themselves as objects rather than loved ones. Kids need to know that they are loved and that this love is unconditional, even if a rule is broken. A necessary balance of love and discipline is not evident in this parenting style. Ephesians 6:4 reads, "Fathers, do not exasperate your children; instead, bring them up in the training and instruction of the Lord."

Style 3: Uninvolved or Negligent

This next style of parenting is basically marked by a lack of involvement. Very little love is evident, and parents feel that discipline is too difficult or time-consuming to carry out. They display a hands-off approach to parenting, setting no limits or expectations for a child's behavior and actions. They provide the basic physical needs—such as food, shelter, and toiletries—but very little emotional support. A child's feelings, emotions, and opinions are irrelevant to these parents.

Two concepts may be at play here. One is that parents are selfish and more concerned with their own trials and tribulations than they are with their children's. They might blame financial stress or suffer from an addiction. Often they have been raised by parents who displayed the same neglectful behavior, and they continue that dysfunctional behavior.

The other possibility is that they haven't embraced the idea of parenting or that they shy away from it because they don't feel they have the tools to parent. Feelings of inadequacy may follow a divorce or a situation that has torn down a parent's self-esteem. Having a child that was unexpected could also lead to shrinking away from the responsibility of parenting.

Whatever the case may be, the chance of a long, lasting relationship for these children is slim, and when they are adults, counseling may be necessary. Hopefully, someone will provide a godly role model for them as they grow and mature. This negligent or inattentive style of parenting is destructive and abusive.

When a person becomes a parent, the circumstances may not be perfect. In fact, there are no "perfect" situations, any more than there are perfect parents. It *is* up to the parents, however, to accept the authority they hold and embrace it. The heart of empowerment is in choosing to use this decision-making control for the betterment of the family. This role may be that of a new parent, a parent of more than one child, a stepparent, a single parent, a new grandparent, and so on. Whatever the situation, biblical authority, according to God's Word, has been rightfully given to the parents or leaders of children. Please accept this challenge and give it your best so that you have no regrets with your children!

Style 4: Authoritarian, Love That Is Balanced with Discipline

Finally, we come to the style of parenting that provides a caring, loving structure and consistent discipline. These parents are humble and totally committed to raising their kids. They understand that this is not an easy endeavor, but they love their children dearly and have chosen to guide and lead them by providing discipline balanced with love.

These parents establish healthy and age-appropriate boundaries, and when kids cross those boundaries, the parents are consistent and willing to explain the reason for punishment. The kids learn respect for their parents at home, and this carries over to other adults, peers, and themselves. As they age, the children learn to monitor their own limits, and while all their decisions may not be the best, they learn from them and develop a sense of independence. After all, isn't it our desire to teach and equip them to be the best adults they can be?

Over the years, these children will develop strong connections and long-lasting relationships with their parents. Such children leave home with self-confidence and good coping skills, along with the ability to control emotions. They are well-adjusted and happy, which enables them to contribute positively to society. Finding proper balance between love and discipline is the goal for authoritarian parents.

One or more of these styles may overlap for you, but this last style—the authoritarian style—has proved, I believe, to be the most effective in rearing children. Please remember that there are no guaranteed ways to raise children. Wonderful children can emerge from lousy parents, and derelict kids can come from responsible, caring parenting situations. However, when love and discipline go hand in hand and are properly balanced, your family will have the best chance for success. Parents are no more perfect than the children they are raising, but when we lovingly work on proper discipline techniques, our children will have the best chance for the future.

Resisting Entitlement

The topic of entitlement deserves a bit more discussion. It is an epidemic in the United States, and we need to understand that this is a battle we should be fighting in our homes! We love our kids, but when a parent crosses the line and goes from being a respected parent to being a friend or confidant, there is a problem.

Kids who feel entitled believe they deserve everything they get. They feel that working for what they receive is not an option. They have received so much perceived "love" that they rarely experience normal feelings like frustration. Parents of "entitled" children strive to make their children happy at all costs, and they go to bat for them when something goes awry. What becomes of these children as adults is not encouraging.

As adults, these individuals tend to be unprepared for the harsh realities this world throws at them. They flounder because the environment in which they live is not always safe and nurturing. They may feel depressed, anxious, and empty inside. They experience turmoil in the areas of relationships, deciding on a career path, and dealing with difficulties.

Those "entitled" individuals who pursue counseling as adults admit that their parents were their best friends, who adored them. Previous generations discussed abuse, neglect, and uninvolved parenting as issues with which they needed help, but today's people are complaining that their parents were too nurturing. They never had to deal with tough situations, and now they are unsure of themselves. Harsh realities are getting the best of them, and now they need help.

In January of 2013, Glen Beck identified four cultural trends that are evident in today's society:

- Self-esteem movement: A dominant feature is that "you are special" and everything you touch is golden. Self-esteem is a good trait, but not when it becomes narcissism.
- Celebrity culture: Reality TV has invaded our lives and dysfunction is selling. Bad behavior is promoted and given too much attention. Consider Justin Bieber and Miley Cyrus.

- Emerging media: People can alter reality, enhance self-promotion, and "fake" who they are. Social media can be a positive communication tool, but it can easily get out of control.
- Credit bubble: We compare what we have to what others have. If we don't have it, we buy it, even if we can't afford it.

If any of these things are out of balance in your home, entitlement may be an issue. Here are five signs that your kids may be feeling entitled, with advice on what parents can do to avoid it.

1. "I want it now." We live in a culture that demands instant gratification and fast food, and drive-through lanes exemplify that. It is okay to say no. Kids do not need everything they want.
2. "I'm not working for that." If children are given everything they ask for, why would they work for it? Sadly, work ethic is lost, and laziness prevails. Give your children little tasks when they are young, and bigger chores or jobs as they get older. We work hard for our money, and so should they.
3. "I'm not cleaning up that mess." This is self-explanatory. When you make a mess, you clean it up.
4. "Everyone else has one." Marketing companies know right where to aim when pitching a product. Children should learn that it is okay *not* to have an item. Worldwide perspective is important, and it teaches us just how much we do have.
5. "Fix it for me." To avoid consequences, parents bail out children too often. A fine line exists between helping a

person and aiding bad behavior or habits. Sometimes your children need to face the music without your help.

Knowing when your children need help and when they can do something on their own is a balancing act for parents. It begins when children are young and continues until they reach adulthood. When we decide to bring children into the world, the goal is to release them as independent beings who are totally reliant on God. From day one, we nurture them in order to achieve this. But here's the thing: when they are capable, let them go! Don't hold on too tightly, because you only know you've succeeded when they leave your home with the tools they need to thrive.

The following event took place very recently. It is a sample of entitlement that made the national news, and it exemplifies what is happening with these children.

The Affluent Influenza Defense: A True Story

For most people, conviction for vehicular manslaughter due to drunk driving warrants a lengthy sentence, but that was not so in the case of Ethan Couch, a wealthy young man from the state of Texas.

The *Fort Worth Star-Telegram* reported that the sixteen-year-old from Keller, Texas, has a rare condition that a judge believes is best remedied by anything other than dealing with the consequences of causing a DWI wreck that killed four people.

According to his lawyers, Couch suffers from "affluenza," a term that means that his wealthy parents pretty much let him get away with everything. The defense saved the boy from a twenty-year sentence when State District Judge Jean Boyd bought the argument at the boy's sentencing on Tuesday. He gave Couch probation instead.

"He never learned that sometimes you don't get your way," Gary Miller, a psychologist assigned to Couch, said in court. "He had the cars, and he had the money. He had freedoms that no young man would be able to handle."

The defense said that this led to a rash of irresponsible behavior on the night of June 15, which ended in tragedy. The spree began with Couch stealing beer from a Walmart with his buddies and ended with his jumping into a pickup truck and smashing into a woman whose car had broken down on a road in Burleson, Texas. He killed the woman as well as a passerby and two people who lived nearby who had come to help. Two teens in the bed of the truck were seriously injured, and one cannot move or talk.

Court testimony revealed that Couch's blood alcohol level was three times the legal limit. Couch admitted being drunk while driving and losing control of his Ford F-150. He pleaded guilty to four counts of manslaughter by intoxication and two counts of assault by intoxication causing bodily injury.

Texas sentencing guidelines for crimes like this call for fines of up to $10,000 and between two and twenty years in the state penitentiary. But instead, Couch got ten years of probation and zero time in prison. If he slips up, he could go to jail for ten years, according to a statement from the Tarrant County District Attorney.

Defense attorney Scott Brown praised Boyd's decision: "She fashioned a sentence that could have him under the thumb of the justice system for the next ten years," he said.

Eric Boyles, who lost his wife and daughter, Hollie and Shelby, in the crash said it was Couch's wealth that kept him from a harsher sentence. "Ultimately today, I felt that money did prevail," he told the *Star-Telegram* after the sentencing. "If [he] had been any other youth, I feel like the circumstances would have been different."

5

Discipline, Discipline, Discipline!

"For the Lord disciplines the one he loves and chastises every son whom he receives. It is for discipline that you have to endure. God is treating you as sons. For what son is there whom his father does not discipline? If you are left without discipline, in which all have participated, then you are illegitimate children and not sons" (Hebrews 12:6–8 ESV).

I originally wanted to write a book that concentrated on discipline. The title would have been something like this: *Discipline: Don't Leave Home without It!* or *Discipline, Discipline, Discipline: A Parent's Best Friend* or *Discipline: Just Do It.* But I believe God led me to address a broader range of parenting skills.

It is my opinion that discipline is a major ingredient of parenting that is lacking or missing today. As followers of Christ, we are disciplined by God, and He expects parents to properly and wholeheartedly discipline their own children. Proverbs 19:18 says, "Discipline your son, for in that there is hope; do not be a willing party to his death." These are convicting words, if you ask me! Discipline is clearly an important part of our growth and a necessary component to parenting.

"Discipline should begin the first day of a baby's life. If you wait until day two, you are one day too late!" This seems a bit extreme, but it was a quote from a popular child psychologist several years ago. The point is that discipline is extremely important, and the sooner you help your child to understand and cope with the rules and expectations around them, the better it is for them. Whether you are married, divorced, separated, or single—no matter what your family situation—unity, clarity, and consistency in discipline will be essential to the child's well-being. The Bible refers to discipline approximately fifty-seven times, so we must take it seriously and commit to growing in this area of parenting.

Love Equals Discipline, and Discipline Equals Love

Discipline is the process of teaching children (and ourselves) which types of behaviors are acceptable and which ones are not. Please, don't ever lose sight of the truth that we discipline our children because we *love* them! In fact, we love them so much that we cannot imagine releasing them into this world without being equipped to deal with the issues of the world. God feels the same, and He provides His Word to guide and lead us. Proverbs 3:11 asserts, "My son, do not despise the Lord's discipline or be weary of his reproof, for the LORD reproves those whom he loves."

As God speaks of the need to discipline, His love is never lost or diminished in the process. It is when discipline is balanced with love that the best results are achieved. Discipline without love will likely fail, for without love in the home, a child will wither like a plant without water. The absence of love has a predictable effect on children.

However, it is not so well-known that excessive love or "super love" imposes hazards too. These children are spoiled by love—or what passes for love.

Before we get started, here are two parenting observations to keep in mind as we discuss discipline. First, I'd like to emphasize that discipline is *not* synonymous with punishment. Discipline is the training that a person receives to correct or mold his moral character and behavior. It might involve punishment (such as time out, loss of privileges, spanking, grounding, etc.), but we cannot overlook the larger aspect of discipline that involves reward and positive reinforcement! Discipline is much more comprehensive than punishment alone. Catch your child doing something good rather than looking only for the negative. Your favor and blessing are important to them!

Second, discipline is one of the most challenging aspects of parenting and leadership in your home. For one thing, the child's age alters your strategies of discipline. What works for a two-year-old will not be effective for a seven-year-old. Also, having more than one child requires a unique strategy for each one, and they must be disciplined as individuals. It is important to regularly review your methods as your children age and mature.

Another challenge arises from the fact that children have different temperaments and personalities. A good friend of mine, Stephen Julian, is an expert in personality identification and methods for working within those areas as they are revealed. Through a series of tests, personalities can be determined. I was curious whether a child's personality could be diagnosed from an early age and the following is his response.

Stephen believes that you can identify a child's personality on the MBTI (Myers-Briggs Type Indicator) scales as follows:

- Extroversion or introversion: If a child has a strong inclination toward one or the other, this can be discerned quite early by social interaction and willingness to go to new people. When a child needs to regain order or rejuvenate himself, does he seek out people, or does he choose to be alone?
- Sensing or intuiting: This can sometimes be seen quite early in the use of language. Does a child play with language, or does he use it quite literally?
- Thinking or feeling: This can be determined fairly early in social interaction. Is the child motivated by "truth" and honest assessments or by tact and being liked (from his perspective, of course)?
- Judging or perceiving: Does the child need a clear schedule for the day? Does she tend to commit to less and get everything done? Or does she commit to more and not worry if deadlines slip?

These basic tenets of personality will cause us to review how we parent our children. Because individuals operate so differently from one another, we must adjust and continually revise our strategies to meet their individual needs.

If you have more than one child, you know that no two siblings respond identically to discipline techniques. The oldest may respond well to one form of discipline, while the youngest does not. Be ready and willing to adjust and grow with each of your children as you discipline them over the years.

Let me add a side note here. There is one thing that never changes with discipline: anger and yelling are not effective ways to deal with children. When children are conditioned to respond only at the peak of a parent's frustration and emotion, discipline becomes useless and exhausting. It is important to establish consistent follow-through on threatened consequences in a calm and judicious manner.

Strategies of Effective Disciplinarians

Feel Empowered

When a baby enters the world, it is the duty and moral obligation of the parents to welcome this new responsibility and commit to the child's well-being. This means accepting the authority you have been given by God and making the choice to raise the child to the best of your ability. This is a short-term privilege because He has only given you a few short years to influence and teach the children. Step one is to embrace this challenge and hold on. The dividends will be well worth it!

Model Respect

The foundation of effective discipline is respect. The child must be able to respect the parent's authority and the rights of others. When this is not present, a child struggles to follow the directions given to them. Matthew 7:12 is the basis for the Golden Rule: "So whatever you wish that others would do to you, do also to them, for this is the Law and the Prophets." Children learn respect when they feel respected.

We must teach them to speak and act kindly and to avoid insults, cruel comments, and rude language when relating to others. We model courtesy and consideration to all family members when we treat others around us properly, regardless of race, sex, age, or ethnic group. We must demonstrate respect for people who do not share our beliefs, likes, or dislikes. Kids will follow our lead! Because respect for the parent, child, and others is so important, I will address it at length later in this book.

Set Clear and Appropriate Boundaries

Discipline is carried out by providing clear and appropriate boundaries. Setting limits and expressing expectations for children help them understand what is expected of them. As they get older, the choices and decisions they make become their own. When these choices are executed successfully, children experience reward or positive consequences. When decisions lead to a failure to meet expectations, negative repercussions are the result.

We went on vacation in Gatlinburg one summer, and Liz and Andy were each permitted to bring a friend. We put guidelines in place for the boys—where they could go, when they should be back, and general "just behave yourself" kind of rules. Two days passed, and all seemed well, until early on the third morning. I went outside to get the paper, and in the entryway stood a four-foot, black, very heavy wooden bear from the resort entrance! I thought to myself, *How did they get that in here? The boys must have snuck out in the middle of the night!*

When I marched into their room, they completely denied that they had done this. However, they did think it was a tremendous idea. When Andy and his friend saw the bear, I sensed that they almost wished they *had* done it.

Questions as to *how* and *when* and *why* circled through my head all morning—until the girls woke up. Liz and Sarah grinned like sleep-deprived Cheshire cats when they entered the room. Suddenly, all my questions were answered when they took full responsibility for kidnapping the bear. My two compliant, reliable, never-do-anything-wrong girls had stolen the bear!

Of course, we made them take it back immediately, and then we proceeded to lay down new guidelines and rules that included them. Looking back now, it was really funny, and we can laugh about it. But we also learned a valuable parenting lesson. *All* children need discipline with clear, appropriate boundaries—even the "easy" ones!

Be Consistent

When a couple brings a child into the world, it is my guess that they rarely discuss the strategies of effective discipline that they will adhere to. Mom and Dad come from two separate family backgrounds, and of course neither will be identical to the other. When they have their own child, they must begin their own methods of discipline. Here's the important thing: it is imperative that you agree on the way discipline will be carried out, and then you must support each other's decisions.

Discipline will flounder if you're inconsistent with it. A child cannot understand when you waver or are lax in applying discipline. If you say something, you must follow through on it every time. Appropriate parental action must take place for your child's sake.

When children get mixed signals, some will play one parent against the other. If Dad is lenient on one thing, or Mom lets them get away with something, they truly do work the system. This causes them not to have a clear understanding of expectations, and it will not promote a healthy marriage scenario. Whatever you do, be united in front of your kids. If discussion is needed, do it later when the children are not around!

Follow Through

Whenever we can provide positive feedback and praise for our children, that is wonderful. However, this is not always possible. When a child disobeys, we must follow through with realistic, age-appropriate consequences and punishments that fit the crime. Be careful of saying something in the heat of the moment that you will regret later. If you say it, you must follow through. This can be more difficult than it sounds.

Here is a true story. Our son was about eleven years old, and the five us were eating dinner one night. I had made fish, and generally everyone liked it, but on that particular night, Andy did not. He made gagging noises and nearly threw up in order to prove to us that he was not going to eat all of his dinner. We became increasingly frustrated with him and insisted that he finish his fish—or he would not participate in his baseball game that night.

Being the strong-willed kid that he is, he sat there for over thirty minutes and refused to finish. Eventually the time came for his baseball game, and we were feeling bad that he would not get to play. Oh, did I mention that it was the last game of the season and he had been selected to play in this all-star game? Guilt overcame us, and we caved. He did not finish dinner; we let him play; and basically he won the parent-versus-child battle. Looking back, we are not proud of that night of parenting, because in that situation, we made a lot of parenting mistakes.

First, the punishment did not fit the crime. Missing an all-star game was a pretty severe punishment, but it came out of our mouths, so we should have stuck to it. Unfortunately, we were not about to keep him from that game, so we did not follow through. The next time he wouldn't finish a meal, we discovered that we had set ourselves up for another possible argument. He knew we'd caved once, and he thought maybe we'd do it again. Sadly, we had made things harder on ourselves that night, but we learned a valuable lesson!

Effective discipline is applied with mutual respect in a firm, fair, reasonable, and consistent way. As parents we strive to protect our children from physical danger and hurtful situations, but this is not our only responsibility. When discipline is balanced by love, our children are prepared for adult issues, and they learn to cope with difficult situations and people. They understand the importance of following rules to avoid negative consequences. When proper boundaries are put in place for children, they can decide their own boundaries and limits as adults. All of these areas help promote healthy relationships for the future. Discipline is not cruel or harsh; it is our God-given responsibility as parents to administer for the well-being of our children.

Strong-Willed Children

Strong-willed kids present a different twist to discipline. It is important to understand that actual discipline techniques may vary, but there is no defining line that separates compliant children from strong-willed children. We all have both sides in us to varying degrees.

A strong will may seem like a negative trait to deal with. However, a truly strong-willed person will go to great lengths to accomplish things that a compliant person may give up on. Strong-willed individuals will let nothing stand in their way!

I mentioned earlier that my son, Andy, is a strong-willed guy. For years we were unsure about how to handle his behavior, and my husband and I were frustrated with our ineffective parenting. He did not sleep through the night until he was five years old. At that time, we bought him a ribbon that said "Sleep Champ!" in hopes that it would encourage him to continue sleeping at night.

Andy also struggled with being apart from us. His separation anxiety was difficult to understand because he was usually going someplace he wanted to go. Whether it involved going into a kindergarten Sunday school class or sleeping over at a friend's house, Andy was not interested. It wasn't until the summer of 2012—when he traveled to Malawi, Africa, for two weeks with a group from our church—that he stepped out of his comfort zone. After he made the decision to go, he told us, "I need to do this on my own." This was a huge step for him.

Our parents often excused Andy's strong-willed behavior, saying that "boys will be boys," but there was more to it than that. His two older sisters were more compliant (even though they had their own issues), so we were stumped. At times, we took parenting skills to a new low—until the term *strong-willed* was introduced to us.

If you suspect that your child is strong willed, then I want to present a few suggestions for you. Please understand that these tips do not apply to children who are merely undisciplined because you have not taken the bull by the horns at an early age. These are strategies that will enhance your relationship with your strong-willed son or daughter and will quite possibly ease some of the tension you may be experiencing.

First, remember that strong-willed children will never respond well to ultimatums. "Do it because I said so" is a loser! They know that you cannot really make them do anything. If they choose not to eat or brush their teeth, for example, they are aware that there will be consequences. But here's the thing: they don't care. They will take whatever punishment you wish to dole out in order to do it their way and in their own time. So, what do we do?

Well, next, we choose our battles. There are spiritual and moral values that must be upheld, along with physical safety issues. These are not negotiable. But if there are instances when you can let something go, do so. Don't make everything nonnegotiable. A favorite saying of mine is this: if everything is important, then nothing is. Agreed?

When Andy was in the fifth grade, we received a phone call from his principal saying that even in the winter months, the kids would be going outside for recess. For most kids, this was not a problem, but Andy refused to wear long pants! The school staff graciously reported that he might get cold, and I kindly replied, "Well, if he does get cold, I hope he is smart enough to wear long pants in the future." Of course, I wanted him to be warm, and I have to admit that I felt like a negligent parent, but if you know our son, you know that this was not a battle worth fighting.

Third, let go of inconsequential matters, but don't let up. It is vital to be very clear about expectations because a strong-willed child will find loopholes in your demands. If it is something that needs to be carried out, then follow through. But if you can have a good laugh over it, do so. At age five or six, Andy had gotten into trouble over something. We were tucking him into bed and were still somewhat upset over his misbehavior, when he said, as seriously as could be, "Mom, you know this is all Adam and Eve's fault. If they hadn't sinned in the garden, I wouldn't have done that." Out of the mouths of babes comes truth!

Fourth, ask questions rather than demanding action. This one can feel like parenting wimpiness. I struggled with this strategy because at times I felt like I was no longer in charge, but it was imperative to lose my own parental pride.

This strategy actually allowed us to maintain authority, but it also permitted our son a share of the control. We said *okay* at the ends of sentences. For example, in a firm voice, we said, "I need you to take the trash out before we leave for your game, okay?" Again, this can be tough, but the request is out there, and they now know what you expect. You are not asking their permission, just reminding them it's a choice.

Fifth, your child always has a choice. While we must choose to stay calm and collected, they must understand that disobedience comes with consequences. We all have choices to make in life. All children have something they do not want to lose. Parents have to work at finding this "button" to push in order to apply a consequence that means something. This incentive will change often as a child ages.

Snuggle time was a fun thing to do before our kids went to bed, but brushing teeth and putting pajamas on was a tenuous process. We learned that by simply saying, "Hey, I hope you get everything done so you have time to snuggle before bed," the children had the choice of getting ready or not. Bedtime was set; they decided their response.

Finally, love for them must always be unconditional. They will consistently pay a price for bad decisions, but losing our love must never be one of the repercussions they suffer. It is our parenting responsibility to protect the relationship at all costs. They may be so frustrated that they tell you to leave or go away, but don't! A strong-willed child will give you your very best moments and your very worst. Love for them is never-ending and cannot be lost.

I hope these few ideas assist you with your strong-willed child. Don't ever feel inept or ineffective when using these more nontraditional styles of discipline. Parenting is not for the faint of heart! There is no exact strategy or guarantee in any form of discipline you choose for your child; there are only guidelines. Honestly, parenting my own children has taken me to my knees so many times, and I am grateful that God hears my cries! He loves our kids more than we could ever love them, so do your best, and enjoy the ride!

Motivating Unmotivated Kids

Motivating our children is another crucial step in the process of their development into successful adults. The book *The World's Most Powerful Leadership Principle* by James C. Hunter asserts that people are motivated to action because they want to act. They want to give their best effort for the team, which in the case of parenting is the family. Hunter claims that, "You get the best effort from others not by lighting a fire beneath them, but by building a fire within them. True motivation is about lighting a fire within people and inspiring and influencing them to action and getting their motor running." Parents cannot change anyone, but they must aspire to influence future choices.

There are different ways to motivate people. Creating a passion in others can be accomplished in one of two ways. The first is the positive way presented through a vision. This form of motivation stimulates people to put out more energy, effort, and enthusiasm. Nick Saban, coach of the University of Alabama football team, says, "Positive motivation gives you a reason and passion to do things you love to do and to push through things you hate." Parents need to establish mutual goals with their children so they have something to work toward. Taking baby steps toward these goals can allow for positive experiences along the way.

Grounding your teenager for an indefinite period of time will not be successful in the long run. Unless they feel as though they have a reason to comply or a goal to reach, most likely they will not even try to do the right thing. They are lost in a sea of teenage despair and cannot visualize the light at the end of the tunnel. Provide them with motivation to achieve, and praise or reward them when they do.

If your teen sasses you or stays out too late, make sure they understand the boundaries or guidelines that you are insisting on. Consequences must be clear and consistently carried out. In a two-parent home, it is imperative that both parents agree in these two areas because a child or teen may target one parent or the other if you do not. Failure to agree can also cause marital strife and division, so be a team and work together for your sake and your children's.

Be willing to listen to your children's feelings and thoughts when they unexpectedly lash out. Something may be churning internally, and it may not even be about you. In fact, it probably isn't. After you talk, you must look for your children to do the right thing, and you must encourage them when they do. "We are to encourage one another," says 1 Thessalonians 4:18. Tiny steps of success, not long-term despair, will help your teen and you to survive these sometimes tumultuous years.

The negative way to motivate people is through unyielding punishment, fear, and guilt. This is a depressing style of motivation, and while it can change current behavior, it will not have long-lasting results. Understanding the difference between discipline and punishment is vital. Remember that discipline changes behavior, while punishment is a one-time response to an action that often results in short-term change. Fear and guilt as motivators have similar results. There is short-term change, but people are less likely to develop long-term commitment and behavior.

Even when it's hard to do, hang in there with your kids. Motivation comes from within; it's personal. As parents, our motivation is to raise our children to love the Lord and to love others. Always remember to find your strength in Him who is able to do all things!

Topic of Debate: Spanking

A topic that is often debated is spanking. It's unlikely that this will ever be settled to everyone's liking. I'd like to propose that no definitive study reveals that spanking has promoted or prompted violence as one ages and then continues on with their own children. Other research and numerous surveys show that more people spank than don't spank. Unfortunately, this is a debate that will go on until the end of time, and my guess is that we will never all agree.

I fall on the side of advocating spanking as an effective way to discipline children—when it is used appropriately and in a loving and fair manner. It should never be a last resort, used in response to bad behavior when other things have not worked and we are at the height of frustration. Spanking should be used only when a child is openly disobedient or defiant. Spilling, toddler tantrums, bed-wetting, or arguing are not proper times to spank. These are normal mistakes and behaviors of children, and in these instances, spanking is not appropriate.

This form of discipline should not be used without clear boundaries that have been set for the child. Also, spanking should not be done in front of others. If you are in a public place, remove the child to a more private setting where others will not be bothered.

Spanking can begin as early as eighteen months of age and usually should not continue past the age of nine or ten. When children understand the word no, they are old enough to spank. Discipline should always be age appropriate, and certainly teenagers are too old to spank. Also, spanking is most effective as a punishment when it is started from an early age for direct disobedience. Starting this at a later age is less effective because a pattern of behavior has already been established.

Here are some guidelines I fully support regarding the use of spanking:

- Never spank when you are frustrated, angry, or out of control.
- Provide one warning, and then be quick and certain of your punishment.
- Be fair, and make sure your actions fit the situation.
- Do not overuse spanking. Use it only for direct and open disobedience.
- Use an open hand over the child's clothing. Never use an object or implement.
- Make sure the child knows you love him/her and that you always will.

Those who are opposed to spanking or any form of capital punishment are entitled to their beliefs. I would be remiss if I did not include a couple of verses that support the biblical view of spanking as a legitimate form of discipline.

"Folly is bound up in the heart of a child, but the rod of discipline drives it far from him" (Proverbs 22:15).

"Do not withhold discipline from a child; if you strike him with a rod, he will not die. If you strike him with the rod, you will save his soul from Sheol" (Proverbs 23:13–14).

When done fairly and lovingly, I believe this is an effective tool, and your child will respect and understand you better. Discipline is teaching, teaching, teaching! There is an old saying: "If your student (or child, in this case) does not learn, you have not taught."

6

Being *the* Role Model to Your Children

"Show yourself in all respects to be a model of good works, and in your teaching show integrity, dignity, and sound speech that cannot be condemned, so that an opponent may be put to shame, having nothing evil to say about us" (Titus 2:7).

Twenty-first-century parents have to compete with multiple sources of information in shaping the minds, values, and beliefs of their children. Unless we have a plan in place, our children will be out in this world without proper and adequate attitudes and mind-sets. Parents must comprehend that they are constantly being watched by their children from an early age on. Even when children become teenagers—though they may not admit it—their parents are the ones to whom they will look for wisdom and leadership. Modeling a life of strong morals and values as well as developing healthy character traits are vital qualities for parents to exhibit.

Children need heroes, or role models, and they are looking for older people to pattern their own lives after. Here is the refrain of a song by the JJ Weeks Band that strongly resonates with me when I consider being a leader or role model for someone:

Let them see You in me.
Let them hear You when I speak.
Let them feel You when I sing.
Let them see You.
Let them see You in me.

"Let Them See You" is one of my favorite songs, and on my way to work in the morning, I sing it at the top of my lungs when it comes on the radio. As I enter into "the world," my heart's desire is to show my colleagues Jesus. The song cries out that we are to take the attention off of ourselves and live our lives so that Jesus is seen. With all my heart, I believe that we, as parents, must show our children Jesus through our actions and words.

Modeling a Jesus-like life is an essential goal, but we all know that He was perfect, and the lives we lead are anything but. Paul said, "I know what I want to do, but I always seem to do the opposite!" (Romans 7:18–19, paraphrased). Even Paul struggled on a daily basis to be more like Jesus.

So how can I make a difference in my child's life? Day in and day out, our children look to us for guidance, and we want to purposefully lead them to the future. So what should we do?

First, we must understand that we are not perfect and will make mistakes. A humble heart allows us to admit mistakes and apologize if necessary. One day, Liz and Andy were arguing over who owned a certain toy. (Beanie Babies were all the rage back then.) To put an end to the squabble, I took over, and eventually I told Andy to give the stuffed toy to Liz and play with something else. Later that evening, I learned it was Liz who had been causing the fuss, and the toy actually belonged to Andy. I apologized to Andy because I had jumped to the wrong conclusion based on past experiences. Humility goes a long way in parenting.

Next, parents must be willing to "walk the walk and talk the talk." If you desire to raise children who love God and others, then you must be mindful of your own actions. Modeling good manners and proper etiquette are positive traits your kids need to observe in you first. On the flip side, a child who hears his parents use crude or inappropriate language may, at the most inconvenient and embarrassing moment, repeat those words they've heard you say. Colossians 3:8 states, "But now you must put them all away: anger, wrath, malice, slander, and obscene talk from your mouth." It is an eye-opening experience when a bad word comes out of a preschooler's mouth!

Third, you are the parent, and you must feel empowered to assume this role, whether you feel ready or not. When parents feel empowered, it means that they have decided to accept the responsibility of raising children and embrace it wholeheartedly. You have authority that demands that you make decisions for your family. Children are God's gift to us, and we must take charge because someone or something is going to guide and influence them. The heart of empowerment is choosing to use this decision-making control for the betterment of the family.

Lastly, parenting and leading our families require us to react properly in the smooth times as well as the difficult situations. For instance, when we react in a stressful situation with calmness and firmness, we are modeling proper responses. Sometimes recognizing that we need a little time to regroup allows our emotions to remain in check.

I was in Walmart one day, and a young woman was shopping with her preschooler, who was sitting in the cart. The child was growing demanding and fussy, and I watched the mom close her eyes, say a little something to herself, and then respond calmly and quietly to the child. It really was terrific!

Throughout the earlier years of raising my children, I was always grateful that our nearby relatives were excited to have a kid or two dropped off at their house, which provided the break I needed. I was able to regain lost composure and then respond to my children in a more calm and sane way. I hope you have avenues in place to give yourself a needed break or "time out."

Role models make impressions—both positive and negative—on other people. In the case of parenting, we focus on our children. They are watching us and listening to us, even when we aren't aware of it. Through character development, teaching and demonstrating social skills, and serving others, we show our families how to live life in a godly manner.

Character Development

A parent who leads effectively in the home should be concerned with character development. Building character greatly matters because character is a moral quality. It stands completely apart from such leadership traits as talent, intelligence, personality, experience, or competence. It is a commitment to do what is right—regardless of circumstances, temptation, hardship, or need.

Andy Stanley says, "It involves doing what is right because it's the right thing to do and there is a standard that is permanent, an unwavering benchmark by which we can measure our choices." That benchmark, of course, is Jesus Christ.

Let's take a look at three character attributes that I believe bolster the lives we are trying to live and model for our families: respect, humility, and morality.

Respect

Developing respect from our children is a critical factor for parents in child rearing. Respect involves developing a feeling of admiration or understanding that someone else is important or is to be taken seriously and should be treated in an appropriate way. We don't encourage this response in order to satisfy our own egos but because respect is the basis for all future attitudes toward other people and self. It is an important family value that will extend outside the home and into school, work, and other social settings. The interaction between a parent and child is the first and most critical one they will have, and any problems or issues experienced there are often seen later in life.

Kids' aren't naturally respectful. When they enter into the world, they are helpless, so parents meet their every need. Babies believe that everyone around them is there to accommodate them and acquiesce to them. As they get older and develop, however, we must help them realize that this is no longer the case. Getting what they want or need is not accomplished by crying, demanding, or fussing. Slowly they learn that other people have feelings too, and little by little, as we model and teach them proper behaviors, they begin to respond accordingly. Children gradually learn that there are other people in the world, that life is not just about them!

There are several ways we can model and teach respect. First, show your kids that you care about their feelings by sympathizing with their needs and comforting their fears. Some of their concerns may seem irrational to you, but they are serious to your children. Don't ever negate their feelings or dismiss thoughts that appear silly to you. You gain their respect when they feel like you are willing to hear them out and listen without judging. They will see you stressing kindness and empathy, and they will learn from this. Praying with them at this point is also a natural way to point them to God as our comforter.

Next, children who grow up in supportive, nonthreatening families are more likely to develop healthy self-respect, which encourages them to believe in their abilities and make good choices for themselves. Taking their feelings into account does not mean that we refrain from correcting and directing those feelings. *Feeling* something doesn't necessarily make it right or accurate. The New Age movement wants you to believe that feelings are truth. I beg to differ.

Rules and boundaries are vital to discipline, and they are also crucial to building respect. Respect includes understanding that we cannot always do things our way. Guidelines are in place to keep us out of harm's way and to maintain order. When we follow and adhere to those guidelines, we hold others in regard, and we learn how to coexist in a peaceful manner.

Related to this is the tension we experience with our rights as humans. The First Amendment of the United States Constitution allows for freedom of speech. Followers of Christ must understand that this does not mean we have the "right" to speak whatever we are thinking. Some people believe that they have the *legal* right to say whatever they want, but they may not have the *relational* right. A respectful person is responsible for the words he utters, and it is a good idea to weigh out possible ramifications before speaking.

James 3:9–10 addresses our speech and warns us about our tongues: "With it we bless our Lord and Father, and with it we curse people who are made in the likeness of God. From the same mouth come blessing and cursing. My brothers, these things ought not to be so."

Another respectful boundary that should be implemented involves the taking, using, or borrowing of a sibling's or parent's possessions without permission. We should not assume that a person is all right with our doing so. Asking permission is the best course of action. Learning to deal with the situation when a person says no is another valuable lesson as well. Girls and clothing seem to be flashing in my mind right now!

Next, we must teach our kids how to express displeasure in an appropriate way when someone, for instance, pesters, interrupts, or disagrees with them. One of the greatest challenges most of us face is how to deal respectfully with people with whom we disagree. Throughout life, this will crop up, and when we model proper ways to deal with conflict, our children will learn a great lesson.

Here are some basic guidelines that you could implement with your children—and put into practice in your own dealings:

- Don't judge people before you get to know them. Treat other people the way you want to be treated. Follow the Golden Rule.
- Listen attentively before you jump in with your argument. We should listen to others' thoughts and ideas when they talk to us, as that creates respect for others.
- Children should be expected to use proper words when communicating with others. Name-calling and bad language are inappropriate and should be dealt with accordingly.
- If you're treated disrespectfully, tell the offending person, "I don't like being talked to that way. Please use a polite tone of voice (or please wait for me to finish speaking) so we can have a discussion."

Children who do not abide by the rules or expectations need consistent consequences. For example, it's confusing to children when we say it's not okay to say a certain word sometimes, but we just laugh at it at other times. Once the boundaries are in place, we must stick to them!

On the other hand, we must compliment our children when they do obey the rules. I like to thank them for using good manners or nice words in a situation. Children respond to positive reinforcement, and they will learn that we respect them and their behavior.

When it comes to respect, TV is not always a good model. Even children's shows can use sarcasm and disrespectful language, so it is important that we are aware of what our kids are watching. As their role models, sometimes we need to watch TV with them and then discuss any discrepancies between our family situations and the show. It sends mixed messages when we allow them to watch something that we do not allow them to do or say. There will also be times when we just have to say, "No, you can't watch that."

When our kids were little, we watched a show called *Rugrats*. It was about the lives of babies and how they filled their days. The oldest Rugrat was Angelica, and she was a spoiled brat. She often bossed around Chuckie, Tommy, and the other babies simply because she could. Angelica was mean and bossy, and we often talked through her behavior, but we also discussed the good behavior of the others. The kids responded well to Angelica's antics, and the story always ended on a happy note. *Rugrats* seemed harmless, as it was a cartoon on the kids' Nickelodeon Channel, but we found many teachable moments within that show!

Finally, our kids need to respect nature and their surroundings. Pets and other animals are wonderful avenues for kids to learn how to take care of and show respect for our four-legged friends. If you walk your dog, take a bag for poo and dispose of it properly. This displays respect for your neighbors' property.

When out enjoying nature, model respect by not disturbing the plants or ripping leaves off the trees because others would like to take pleasure in them as well. We should never leave trash at a sporting field without putting it into a trash can. Genesis 1:26 is our mandate to protect the earth: "Then God said, 'Let us make man in our image, after our likeness. And let them have dominion over the fish of the sea and over the birds of the heavens and over the livestock and over all the earth and over every creeping thing that creeps on the earth.'"

Some parks and many schools and businesses today have recycling bins. Learning to recycle has made a huge difference to the environment since it took off in the 1970s. Attention and awareness of the positive impact of reuse and recycling was highly emphasized at that time as energy costs began to soar. We've learned that significant energy savings are obtained when glass, paper, and scrap metals are reused and recycled.

It is important that kids learn to feel that they are part of their neighborhoods and that they take ownership in it. Picking up trash, planting flowers and trees, supporting neighborhood cleanups, and recycling are wonderful ways that kids can learn to respect nature and to contribute with those around them.

Teaching and modeling respect is so important for parents to embrace. Children learn how to be respectful at an early age, and these lessons begin at home. Each day as they continue to grow and mature, respect will become a part of their DNA.

Humility

"Do nothing from selfish ambition or conceit, but in humility count others more significant than yourselves" (Philippians 2:3).

Modeling humility is another very important aspect of parenting. Parents who are humble will stand firm for core values and beliefs, and they are a joy to be around. They are so entrenched in the fact that God is in control and leading their lives that they are fun, relaxed, and uplifting. They do not put on airs of being better or more important than anyone else. They simply trust God to lead them and their families.

Humble parents tend to avoid exaggeration, and they live life with realistic expectations. Have you ever met parents who incessantly ramble on about their kids, while in reality they are hiding some very deep-seated troubles? They portray their children as perfect little angels who can do no wrong. I am here to tell you that those types of children do not exist. We are all born with a sin nature, and no matter who we are, we will have difficulties. It's sad to say, but some church families are notorious for how they look on the outside, when, on the inside, they are a train wreck!

Humble parents examine who they are, and they are willing to make changes to adjust to situations that are not going well. This flexibility is not threatening to their authority because they understand that God is ultimately in charge. We cry out to Him for help and patience and support because without God, we may be inclined to think we are in control.

Humility develops strength in children that they may not be aware of. There is no weakness in being a humble person, even when it sometimes means apologizing for mistakes. On several occasions, I've had to ask for forgiveness when I've overreacted to a situation and have said things I shouldn't have said to my husband or children. Other times, we have learned to laugh at our own mistakes and move on. Learning to laugh at yourself is an underrated skill, in my opinion.

Kids will see you as confident when you encourage those around you and celebrate their victories with them. Several times a year, you hear a story about a parent who does not understand humility when it comes to watching their child play sports. Fights break out in the stands, as hostile parents dislike the coach, the referee or umpire, or another parent. Parents lose perspective, and these situations cause embarrassment and humiliation for children. Learning to lose graciously and win gracefully are sometimes lost in the name of competition. A humble parent is not threatened by encouraging other people.

Self-confidence or self-esteem must be used to balance humility. We cannot go around being pitiful and acting as though we are weak and uninspired. Self-confidence simply means that, as effective parents, we have a position of authority, but at no time should we let our egos get in the way. Self-assured parents understand that what they are doing makes a difference in their child's life.

It is crucial for parents to model a balance between humility and self-confidence. Confidence can be a fragile commodity, especially for youth and teens. Schoolwork gets tougher, hormones are extremely active, friends can be unreliable or temporary, and general self-esteem issues make confidence difficult at times. Proverbs 3:5–6 tells us to "trust in the LORD with all your heart and lean not on your own understanding; in all your ways acknowledge him, and he will direct your paths." We won't always understand why things are happening, but we can have full assurance that He is leading the way!

Challenges will be before our children throughout their lives, and parents must find positive ways to encourage and motivate them. As they learn to believe in themselves, they also learn that they are made in the image of God and that He wants them to succeed. Humility and self-confidence in balance promote not only success for the future but rationality and reason in the moment.

Morality

Modeling morality means showing your children the difference between right and wrong behavior. Consider yourself the modern-day Aesop. Throughout childhood and beyond, we must teach morals to our children so they learn valuable lessons for life. Some morals are learned in the wonderful times of life, but some are taught through hardship. The Bible tells us that in this life we *will* have trouble, and as parents we must use these teachable moments to help our children grow. They are watching how we respond to good and bad. The following are a few of the traits we must teach our children without fail.

I'd like to start with *integrity*. A person of integrity is always the same person, whether he's in public or private, at home, at school, at work, alone, or being watched by others. People with integrity are trustworthy, and if they promise something, they will do it. Their actions are based on high moral principles. Proverbs 10:9 says, "Whoever walks in integrity walks securely, but he who makes his way crooked will be found out." Integrity issues frequently arise between you and God, as He is quite often the only one who knows what you are doing and what your motives may be.

Job, in the Old Testament, was a man of integrity. He suffered much pain and loss, yet he held firmly to God. Job 2:9 reads, "Then his wife said to him, 'Do you still hold fast your integrity? Curse God and die.'" Job's own wife was encouraging him to abandon his faith. Later in 27:1–6, Job picked up his discourse and again refused to speak against God. Job was a godly man of integrity, even through extremely trying circumstances. It is vital that parents model integrity for their children.

Modeling and speaking with *honesty and truthfulness* are moral character traits that leaders of the home must never waver from. Truth and honesty with children, as well as other adults, are essential qualities, even when circumstances are difficult or uncomfortable. Seemingly harmless, little white lies or lies of omission can lead to disaster! When children do not tell the truth, they often do so to avoid punishment or negative consequences. I believe that adults do it for the same basic reason.

Parents who understand that there is only one truth are not only teaching their children an important virtue, but they are also pointing those children to God. Today's world wants you to think that you create your own truth. People may not believe the Word of God, but that does not make it any less true. John 1:14 says, "And the Word became flesh and dwelt among us, and we have seen his glory, glory as of the only Son from the Father, full of grace and truth." Jesus brought us truth, so let's make sure our kid's understand it!

Kindness, gentleness, and *caring* are moral qualities that men and women alike should portray and model for their family. Each one displays an attitude that removes the focus from self and places it onto others. Women do not corner the market on these traits. Men need to realize that their daughters are looking to the primary male figure in their lives when considering a spouse.

These are not the only qualities daughters observe, but they are important to them. None of these three characteristics imply softness or weakness. It takes much strength and conviction to care for others in a gentle and kind manner. One of my favorite quotes comes from the movie, *Radio*: "It's never a mistake to care for someone. That's always a good thing."

My son was in middle school when he met a boy named Kevin. Kevin, who has Asperger's syndrome, was new to the district, and Andy took to him immediately in homeroom. It wasn't until we went to our first middle school conference that we learned of this relationship. Apparently, Andy, who is quite athletic, told his gym class that if the team captains wanted him on their teams, then Kevin came with him. They were a package deal. He wanted Kevin to fit right in and to know how important and valuable he was as a friend. Kevin was never the last one picked throughout middle school, and to this day, he and Andy still have a close relationship.

Parents or leaders promote *diligence* and a *strong work ethic* in their children, who then strive for excellence in their own work. They fight off morally wrong laziness and sloppiness. They are self-starters and act productively and decisively, without having to be told what to do. Proverbs 13:4 states, "The soul of the sluggard craves and gets nothing, while the soul of the diligent is richly supplied." I believe that these are points of contention among recent adults heading into the work force. Is it an important emphasis in your home?

Finally, I want to implore the teaching of *fair-mindedness*, not just fair play. Fair-mindedness is teaching your family to treat all people equally and without regard to such superficial distinctions as class, gender, race, and so on. Along with this goes the willingness to put up with others and their ideas, even if we do not like or agree with them. The end will come when all tribes and nations have heard the good news, and we will all worship our heavenly Father together. Somehow, some way, we must all learn to get along.

My guess is that the importance of instilling these values in your children did not come as a surprise to you. As a mom of three, I know that teaching these areas is important, but somehow the world gets in the way. If it's so obvious, why is bullying such a prominent and unfortunate issue? Why do teens drink and kill themselves and others? With one week left in the month of January 2014, several random shootings have made the national news already this year. Why? Darkness is among us, my friends. But take heart. Jesus has overcome the world, and He is our hope, now and forever!

Social Skills

Children are not born with social knowledge or social skills, and they eagerly look for someone to imitate. At a very early age, infants connect with someone near them through eye contact, voice recognition, and familiar touch. That "someone" is usually one or both parents. We are a child's first teacher and role model, and usually children are more affected by what their parents do than by what their parents say. They learn how to behave by seeing how their mothers and fathers behave around others and by following their example.

Social skills are those communication, problem-solving, decision-making, self-management, and peer-relations abilities that allow one to initiate, build, and maintain positive social relationships with others. In other words, social skills affect how we interact with those around us, including family, friends, or other children and adult-child relationships. Research shows that parents play a significant role in the development of these skills.

For example, if we desire that our children behave properly in public, we must prepare them well in advance. Manners seem to be a somewhat lost social skill these days, in my opinion, and I am saddened by this. Sitting at the dinner table at home is a great place to start teaching manners. If you allow your children to run around with snacks or lunch items at home, then don't expect them to sit quietly at a restaurant. It is important for them to hear you use words such as *please, thank you, excuse me,* and *may I*. Politeness was once an expectation for our children, but unfortunately, it is slowly becoming a lost art. Please find value in teaching your children manners from an early age!

Jon, Andy, and I were in line at *Chipotle* one day, when I observed a family of five eating lunch. The kids were probably around the ages of five, three, and one. Mom was assisting the baby with her food, while Dad interacted with the older children. To the parents' credit, the meal appeared to be quite enjoyable and peaceful. I was so pleased to see this happening that I had to compliment the adults on their parenting skills and the children for their good behavior. The other people around them calmly enjoyed their dining experience too.

This success story does not occur without much hard work in the home. There was an expectation that they were there to eat and spend time together. The parents did not choose a restaurant where the kids would be asked to wait for a seemingly long period of time before the food arrived. Proper manners were modeled and conveyed to the children, and respect was shown to the people around them as they ate. I loved it!

Identifying Necessary Social Skills

Making friends and then interacting with them is a worthy place to start when a child is learning social skills. From a young age, children need opportunities to interact with other children, especially those their own age. Parents can assist by having friends over, joining a play group, attending Sunday school, or meeting other children in the neighborhood. Promoting and then overseeing peer interaction is a worthwhile activity, even at a young age.

When children come together, they must learn how to get along. This skill does not come naturally for all children. Sharing can be the first step in the process. I have worked in our nursery with toddlers between the ages of twelve months and two years. At that age, they are walking and can talk to get their points across. There are toys everywhere, but for some reason, only a few are the favorites. This is the beginning of learning to deal with others through sharing—and using words instead of hitting.

Typically, the twenty-month-olds are way more domineering than the thirteen-month-olds, so it is necessary to help them understand why they can't just grab toys away or strike another child who doesn't hand it over. Sometimes, merely directing them to another toy or other form of distraction does the trick. Feelings may get hurt, but they are learning. Interestingly, you can often tell which children either have siblings at home or have parents who have previously dealt with this. Saying they are "sorry" is essential too.

Around age four or five, children learn to interact together rather than merely sitting next to each other as they play individual games or participate alone in an activity. As they interact, children learn to take turns, wait patiently, and not interrupt each other when talking. During these preschool years, your children should be learning fundamental yet lifelong skills. Standing in line and staying in one's own space are social skills that we use all of our lives.

I also feel that children around this age should be choosing their own clothes and dressing themselves. Tops and bottoms may not always match, but that is not the point. They are learning to be independent.

During the elementary ages, kids can really dig into problem-solving. A parent is wise to allow a child to work through an issue and, whenever possible, to think through the problem himself. Listening to a situation without always trying to solve it helps the child grow and mature. We are being supportive when we can help them figure things out on their own. Sometimes we need to step in, but we must be mindful of times when listening is more effective than speaking and telling them what to do.

Middle school is notorious for dealing with hardships with friends, coping with bullies, and understanding feelings that change rapidly. Relationships can be tenuous, and emotions can run high. A parent continues to nurture and support social skills taught earlier in life and understands that boundaries must be in place. Maintaining the use of appropriate language and respect for the parent is crucial. You may feel as though your parenting is in a downward spiral at times, but learn not to take everything your teen says personally. During those years in our house, Jon and I frequently reminded ourselves of a saying we'd heard: "If everything is important, then nothing is." Sometimes parents have to pick their battles.

All through the teenage years, we must continue to take advantage of teachable moments. Often, that means speaking truth into a situation that has gone bad or has turned an unexpected direction. Peer pressure can wreak havoc with a teen who does not know the difference between right and wrong. When our children succumb to bad decisions, it is vital that they learn from them, rather than make the same mistakes over and over.

The actual time we can spend with our teens is limited, compared to when they were younger. Because of activities, friends, school, and a number of other reasons, we see our teens less, so we must schedule time with them and be adamant and intentional about communicating and staying on top of things. Their friends will become more and more influential as the years pass. Time will be short, and when all is said and done, we must embrace, cherish, and welcome our responsibility to model and teach our children for as long as we can.

Abby made the dance team in her freshman year of high school. Practices began in the summer before school started, so I found myself dropping off my fourteen-year-old for this new adventure called high school. She was as confident as she could be, but I was a nervous wreck. The parking lot we drove through had several other activities going on, such as band practice, cross country, and football warm-ups. I remember thinking that the students looked so old!

As she got out of the car, a tear came to my eye. My firstborn was growing up, I thought to myself, and I watched her walk in. I slowly pulled away, and with tears streaming down my face, all I could do was cry out to God, "Please, Lord, I pray that I did all I could do as her parent!" I knew our relationship was growing and changing, and how I would parent her from now on would be different. Time was truly flying by, and for the first time, I believed it.

Serving Together

"As each has received a gift, use it to serve one another, as good stewards of God's varied grace: whoever speaks, as one who speaks oracles of God; whoever serves, as one who serves by the strength that God supplies—in order that in everything God may be glorified through Jesus Christ. To him belong glory and dominion forever and ever. Amen" (1 Peter 4:10–11).

No matter the age of your children, volunteering together as a family is a great way to spend quality time together while shaping your child's character. There are hundreds of ways to volunteer together as a family—from preparing or serving meals, to doing yard work, to going on local and international mission trips.

There are several advantages to serving together. First, it promotes family support and communication. These are times when parents and children can share feelings and thoughts openly. Serving together allows parents to be positive role models to their children, and it cultivates proper attitudes toward helping others. It forms a child's identity and a sense of purpose, and it helps children grow up to be more caring and responsible toward other people. Modeling appropriate behaviors and attitudes for our children will have long-lasting benefits.

One of my favorite times with Abby was when I was a chaperone on a trip to Green Bay, Wisconsin, when she was in middle school. We worked at a local Salvation Army and helped local people with outdoor work and cleaning. Students from all over the area came together to serve the people of Green Bay. This present week, Abby is in New Orleans, leading a team of students on a stateside mission assignment for YWAM. I had a feeling, even back when Abby was an eighth-grader, that she would be serving others in some capacity.

Not all opportunities for serving together have to be time-intensive. Liz and I used to prepare meals or baked goods for friends and acquaintances in need. This was a wonderful time we shared, and I loved having her help me in the kitchen. Today, along with her fiancé, Andrew, and others in their church, she helps lead a ministry to prepare and deliver small "care packages" to homeless folks on the streets of Los Angeles. Liz is always first to pass on a caring word and to demonstrate the love of God to them.

Serving is a wonderful way to contribute to your community and surrounding area. As I was getting ready for work, the morning news ran this story on January 6, 2014. A dad was using his snowblower to clear his neighbors' driveways and sidewalks. He said that a group of men he knew had decided to expand their grass-cutting services to include shoveling snow for neighbors in need. The camera scanned to his seven-year-old daughter, who was shoveling snow little by little. The reporter asked, "Why are you doing this?" She simply said, "I'm helping them. Who else is going to do it?" To her, serving just seemed like the right thing to do.

Research shows that children who serve others with their parents, or who observe their parents giving to others, are more likely to serve or volunteer when they become adults. Jesus modeled service and encouraged his followers to serve others the way He did—without expecting anything in return. Matthew 20:28 says we are to serve, "even as the Son of Man came not to be served but to serve, and to give his life as a ransom for many."

When children serve with their parents, they are empowered. They feel as though they are making a difference in the world. Don't let the world guide and lead them astray, but take the initiative and be their role model. Jesus Christ set the bar, and now we are to follow His lead.

Lord, let our actions and words be pleasing to You!

7

Communication Required

Communication is a tool we use to establish and modify relationships. It is a two-way street where people convey their thoughts, feelings, instructions, information, and so on to make connections with other people. The process is best accomplished when the communication is clear and accurate. The goal of effective communication for families is to find a healthy balance between your intellect (thinking) and your emotions (feelings) in order to transfer information from one person to another.

We often think of communication in relation to work and education, but it is critical in the area of family relationships too. Those closest to us can bring out the best and worst of our emotions, and it is during those times that proper communication is vital. We've all had experiences where we've felt that we were heard and understood, but most of us have also felt misunderstood and maybe ignored. When communication is presented well, the family unit finds itself in a much better state than it does when communication is missing or done poorly.

As with most components of parenting, communication is a dynamic area. Little ones need you to get down on their level and communicate simply and concisely. Hold their little faces and ask them to look you in the eyes before you try to provide directions. They can only comprehend so much. Be clear about your expectations and the consequences for not meeting them, and then make sure the child understands you. As always, you must follow through.

When children get older, more distractions come into play when communicating. Toddlers and preschoolers tend to be closer to parents in physical proximity, while older children might be in another room reading, watching TV, doing homework, or playing outside with friends. We have all attempted to give instructions or information to our children when they were not completely engaged, and then we were met with virtually no response. Others of us may give directions, knowing full well that the child will not comply the first time because we always say something three or four times before getting serious. Remember that communication is a two-way street. Talking to someone who is not listening is doomed to fail.

Finally, communicating with teens is a crucial responsibility for parents. Here, I believe it is extremely important that communication does not break down before it starts. Time with our teens is short, so we must be willing to put our agendas aside to listen to what our children have to say. At this stage of parenting, if we do not make an effort and show them respect by listening, our teens may very well stop coming to us altogether.

Consummate Communication

We will address three basic areas of communication, and then I will present some communication barriers that may exist within our families. First is the area of nonverbal communication better known as body language. Second is active listening, which is different from simply hearing when interacting with someone. And third, is stress management, which allows us to be effective when we convey our thoughts and feelings. Each of these topics will suggest ways to show respect and nurture your relationships, which will help you connect with your children as they grow and mature. This is crucial. If kids can discuss the little things with you, then they are more likely to come to you for the big stuff down the road.

Nonverbal Communication

First, we must understand that communication is not always a spoken word. Emotions, feelings, body language, past experiences, and many other factors play into our children's ability to translate and understand what is being relayed to them. Parents must learn to read these signs to be effective. Some research says that way over half of the information we transfer is accomplished through nonverbal cues, so in essence, *not* communicating *is* communicating. This is why face-to-face interaction is so much more productive than texting, e-mail, and so on.

When communicating with our children, eye contact conveys an interest in what the child is saying, and it allows us to focus on their words. This sign of respect encourages conversation, as everything else happening around you is set aside. If you must finish what you are doing, look at your child and ask if you can continue your conversation in a few moments. Your facial expressions must adequately and consistently show interest as well. Have you ever known anyone who could simply "give the look" to communicate a hundred words?

Appropriate posture is also necessary to convey accurate information. An open stance with your arms at your sides says that you are approachable, but crossed arms and hunched shoulders suggest disinterest in the conversation or an unwillingness to engage. Hands on your hips can transmit a negative feeling of disapproval, so be mindful of this as well. Children need to feel that you take them seriously, and proper posture is either inviting or withdrawn and defensive in nature.

Hand gestures or even a pat on the back can speak volumes in a conversation. Large movements express adamant and strong emotions but can be intimidating to a child. Subtle and small gestures can accomplish big things. A nod of the head or a pat on the back can communicate affirmation, just as shaking your head no can reflect disapproval. The older your children are, the better they become at reading these nonverbal cues, and vice versa. Be careful of unspoken, inaccurate communication because our children are very aware.

Active Listening

Becoming a proficient and successful listener begins by understanding that listening is not the same as hearing. As I sit here and write these words, I can hear the wind chimes blowing in my backyard, and the wind whooshing through the trees as the rain hits our roof. I am aware of the storm outside, but I am not engaged with it. Active listening will make your child feel heard and understood.

Listening requires an effort on our part to understand and participate in a two-way transmission of communication. Active listening lets others know that we are working to understand the message they are sending. We ought to create an environment that allows for expression of ideas, opinions, and feelings. Freedom to plan and to solve problems creatively lets your children express themselves without fear of rejection or ridicule.

Again, reduce any distractions that will keep you from focusing on your child's message. Try to stop whatever you are doing that may distract you from his message, such as watching television or trying to read while he is talking to you. Attempting to listen while doing another task usually does not allow a parent to clearly hear the message. Sometimes it is best to find a quiet or less busy place if the seriousness of the conversation dictates that you do so.

As mentioned previously, when we are engaged and not distracted by other things, our body language conveys to our children that we are interested and listening. We make eye contact with them, turn our bodies toward them, and nod as they are talking—all of which let them know that we are actively listening. We must not interrupt or project our thoughts until they are finished talking, as this is rude and detracts from the messages they are conveying.

Next, listen for the meaning and emotions behind the words. Don't just listen to the *content* of what is being said. Listen for the *feeling* that your child is trying to convey to you. Is your child expressing joy, sadness, excitement, or anger through their words or body language? Parents understand and interpret their children's feelings and emotions better than anyone else, so read the entire message, not just the words.

After your child has finished talking, paraphrase back to them what you've heard. "What I am hearing from you is …" or "It sounds like … was very upsetting for you." The child first needs to know that you have understood them and that they have sent their message clearly to you. Clarifying the information helps to avoid conflict in the future and corrects any misunderstandings.

When children have been heard, it produces calmness within them. Whether they are confessing the truth about an issue (John 8:32 says that "the truth will set you free"), expressing deep frustrations, or simply talking about their day, you will be surprised at how your conversations and relationships change as you focus and listen to them. When you give your children an opportunity to open up to you, everyone benefits. After all, active listening will go a long way for them in adulthood.

Managing Stressful Situations

This section is not meant to single out teenagers, but as our kids age, the levels of engagement will change. When children are young, our stress is primarily physical in nature because we are extremely busy and active in meeting their needs. Getting kids dressed, lifting them into car seats, playing on the floor, changing diapers, and cutting up food are only a few examples of the physical workout parents go through each day. Children rely on their parents to keep them safe and happy. I always say that God gives babies and toddlers to young adults because they have *way* more energy to keep up with the little ones!

As children age, our parenting becomes more mentally challenging. We must begin to help them grow and mature through our words and behaviors rather than doing everything for them. We strive to teach them independence without totally letting go. Still, parents must maintain appropriate discipline and follow through. The fact is that the older a child gets, the bigger the problems will be. Fussing at the grocery store turns into arguing over car privileges, and early morning wake-ups turn into late-night curfews. I love how God prepares us every step of the way to handle life as it comes!

So, our kids become teenagers, and we try our best to communicate with them, but sometimes it seems like a struggle. To manage stressful encounters, start by recognizing that you are stressed. At such times, it may be wise to consider talking at a later time, when both parties have calmed down. Sometimes parents and children or teens need space and time before effective communication can take place.

When the time is right, go back to the situation and calmly discuss the issue. Waiting does not mean forgetting or avoiding a conversation that needs to take place. Tough conversations must be thought through carefully. Consider what you want to say or what questions you need to ask. It is crucial to have a plan to make a difficult conversation go as well as possible.

If the situation does not permit a break, take a few deep breaths and ask God for wisdom for the moment. He is the source of all wisdom, and He will provide you with peace and guidance in the heat of the moment, if you allow Him to. There will be times when a compromise is necessary, or you may need to agree to disagree. This does not mean that you're relinquishing your authority and rights as a parent. It simply means that your thoughts and opinions differ. Consequences for wrong behavior or actions are still carried out in love.

Heated or stressful confrontations must never lead to a severing of the alliance between parent and child. It is your responsibility as the parent to maintain the relationship at all costs! Respect, love, and truth are foundational, and when they are displayed properly, difficult situations and issues are not devastating. Ephesians 4:15 directs us to "speak the truth in love." Our children may not always like what we are communicating, but in hardship or happiness, we must respond as did our perfect model, Jesus Christ.

Barriers to Effective Communication

Never:

- use sarcasm, a crabby voice, hostile criticism, or cutting remarks.
- say *always* or *never.*
- insinuate that you know what your children are thinking. Let them complete their thoughts.
- deny or refuse that a problem exists.
- bring up old arguments.
- get defensive. Often the problem is not even about you.
- overwhelm your child with too many words. This is construed as nagging or lecturing, and tuning out is often the response.
- listen only so you can say what you're thinking. Avoid formulating your response instead of listening to the child.
- try to "top" their feelings with your own. Deal with your issues separately.
- overreact. Yelling, aggression, and rejection are never effective communication skills.
- underestimate the seriousness of your child's anxieties.
- feel as though you *must* respond. God gave us two ears and one mouth, so listen twice as much as you talk.
- fix a problem that your children can fix themselves. Guide and encourage the solution, but don't take over.

- forget that God is with you and loves your children even more than you do!

No doubt, communication is important for the health of your family. Parents need to constantly be on the lookout for open times to communicate without distractions. This will be the best time for your children to receive instruction, share information, or just plain catch up on things. Take advantage of one-on-one time, and listen to their every word. Our Abby was most interested in sharing at night before bed. All of the day's events seemed to come flooding out, and it was sometimes difficult to stay focused because I was tired, but this was a necessary and special time of sharing with her.

Liz is, to this day, still an early bird and a healthy eater. I always knew that she alone would be up in the morning, eating a sensible breakfast. I was intentional about meeting with her at that time to discuss upcoming events or activities and to share any other important information. (I feel certain that she didn't even realize that I did it.) That was our uninterrupted time before the day began.

Finally, Andy's best time to communicate was in the car while going somewhere. It was the most effective time to hold his full attention and eliminate distractions. As he grew older, Andy also shared at night, and I was grateful that our communication continued. Once your kids start driving, you will miss the interaction that occurs while you're driving them from place to place. Enjoy that time in the car together. You'll be glad you did.

I appreciate what Jon Gordon, a businessman, once said: "Communicate with transparency, authenticity, and clarity. No matter how busy your day may be, touch base on a regular basis. The truth is, you can't afford not to." This is so true!

Technology and the Family

Technology, along with the Internet, has opened doors of communication that today's parents must be aware of. Unfortunately, children may find it easier to lay their lives out in cyber space than to express themselves to a family member. Technology and social media seriously impact the family unit, but is that good or bad?

Like it or not, children's absorption with technology, from texting to playing video games, does by its very nature limit their ability to communicate with their parents. What has transpired is independence in communicating with friends and other people. We no longer share a common phone in the house, where Mom or Dad can pick it up and know who's calling. Our children's friends now sit in the car and text that they have arrived, so we no longer interact with those friends face-to-face. Recent technology inventions have eliminated avenues that allow parents to monitor their children's social lives.

This new independence from parents at an earlier age through mobile phones, instant messaging, and social networking can create a divide—or a type of freedom from the "helicopter" parent that a child sees as intrusive. Parents on the other hand see it as a loss of connection with their child and an inability to provide oversight to safety issues and overall, healthy well-being.

Children and teens use many forms of technology, but parents are equally guilty in distancing themselves from their kids. The mobile "smart phone" allows adults to talk, check e-mail, watch videos on the Internet, and do other things, when they could be connecting and sharing with their families. Some parents also might use technology to relinquish their duties by setting their kids in front of a video or television program. I must admit that

I was guilty of that a time or two. The bottom line is that we make choices every day about the ways we will communicate with our children, and we determine their use of technology as well. You are in charge, so take time to review the quality of communication in your household.

As challenging as it may seem, parents must be proactive in learning about and becoming informed of the information out there. When I say "out there," I'm talking about the cyber world. I, for one, struggle to keep up with the latest advancements in technology as well as social media, but I am grateful that my husband is more in tune with it. Parents today struggle to gain proficiency and comfort with the new technology that kids have already mastered, and those parents are likely to ask their teenagers for information regarding these areas. Where did this all begin?

Technology Advancements at a Glance

The development of the Sony Walkman in the early 1980s was a huge step in sound technology and the playing of music. It was the first portable and private sound device that you could carry with you. With headphones on each ear, the individual was able to shut off the outside world like never before. This created a whole new era regarding technology and communication.

Prior to that, there were telephones and radios (invented in 1890 and 1891 respectively), which actually brought people together. Telephones allowed people to communicate in their own voice a message that previously had to be written and carried to others. Sitting around the radio, listening to newscasts and entertaining shows with family and neighbors, became a unifying event for the ages. These technological advances for transmitting sound and the human voice were the beginning of many inventions yet to come.

It wasn't until 1974 that the first personal computer was developed and made available in the United States. It was extremely expensive, and families rarely owned one. But in 1984, Apple created the Macintosh computer, and the average family was able to afford a home computer. Since that time, other innovations have come into existence.

- 1990: the beginning of the World Wide Web
- 1995: the first DVD
- 1996: Nokia's best-selling mobile phone
- 2001: the Palm Pilot or PDA
- 2003: Facebook
- 2005: YouTube
- 2006: Twitter and Blackberry (also known as Crackberry because of its addictive nature)
- 2007: the first iPhone
- 2011: mass-produced smart phones

This is only a slight glimpse of technology and social media growth that has consumed our families in the last twenty-five years. Can you imagine the growth that will take place in the future?

The Bible compels us to meet together in person. Hebrews 10:24–25 reads, "And let us consider how to stir up one another to love and good works, not neglecting to meet together, as is the habit of some, but encouraging one another, and all the more as you see the Day drawing near." We are reminded in 1 John 1:1–2 that God did not send us a Savior through social media or the Internet. He sent Jesus to be with us.

So, what are some steps we can put in place for the betterment of our families regarding technology and social media?

Here are some suggested boundaries and/or guidelines for using technology and social media.

First, don't allow iPods, handheld video games, or headphones at the table, in the car, or in the middle of a conversation. One study shows that 93 percent of success in a conversation is determined through nonverbal indicators. We miss out on so much when we are not face-to-face with the person we wish to communicate with.

Second, arrange regular periods of time with no technology. It was not so long ago that this was not an issue, so there is not much evidence on how it will affect our families in the future. Do you ever wonder why we would miss technology so much if we suddenly lost it? Could it be because technology is habit-forming? We constantly check our phones or computers for any missed information or new updates. I once heard that the average person looks at his phone an average of two hundred times a day. Wow! It seems that we must be using it not only for our practical needs but also to prevent or relieve boredom because that is a lot of looks!

My friend Chelsea went to Haiti in the summer of 2013. She had never been on a short-term mission trip before, so she felt a bit of apprehension, even though God had clearly moved her heart to go. I will never forget the day when she came over and told us about her trip. The first thing out of her mouth was how much she appreciated the simplicity of the country. She did not miss the hectic pace we set for ourselves in the United States. The joy exuded by the Haitian children was not over a game or a new iPad. It was a response to the relationships they had with those around them. Wouldn't we all like a simpler, less hectic life at times?

Third, place limits on the time spent watching TV and playing computer/video games, especially if it is not educational. Cable television and the computer have opened a new door to ill-reputed influence that enters our homes. Here are a few questions you should be mindful of for your children's sake: Are the things they're watching respectable and not sending mixed messages about right and wrong? Am I fully aware of the content of the things my kids are watching and playing? Would God be pleased with my choices of entertainment?

Discussing shows you watch together is a good idea. Teachable moments come in many forms, and asking your children what impacted them may provide unexpected answers. Even a PG movie these days can contain inappropriate viewing for a youngster. The website www.pluggedin.com provides movie reviews you may find helpful.

Finally, I highly recommend not allowing your children to have a TV or computer in their bedrooms. Not only should they have a place where they can wind down and be still, but it is extremely difficult to monitor and guide what they are doing. When children escape to their rooms to play video games or watch TV, parents are less able to model healthy behaviors and share positive values, and effective communication can be obstructed.

Love is the most necessary attribute to show in person whenever possible, but technology and social media are not all bad. They have opened doors for communication like we have never experienced before. Facebook allows me to see pictures and hear stories that my kids post from all over the world. I can call or text them without hesitation, and they can do the same.

Many of you have never even heard of calling cards, but they contained "minutes" and were used to make long-distance phone calls back in the day. In the past, I had to set up a time, usually on Sundays, to call home from college to speak to my parents. Spontaneous and unexpected calls often led to disappointment because phones were only in homes, not carried everywhere with us.

Today I am grateful for the advances in technology that have opened up avenues of communication with my own children that never existed before. Through social media, I have reconnected with classmates I haven't seen in years and with family members I'd lost touch with. All in all, it's a satisfactory way to stay in touch with others.

Keep in mind that most kids themselves cannot afford to buy the technology available today, yet we still have issues. Parents must step up and pursue what is appropriate for them and their children. Determine guidelines, and help your family find balance in the world of technology and social media.

8

Spiritual Disciplines and Emerging Faith

I recently heard this quote: "You can't teach what you don't know." This snippet applies to many areas of life, but in relating to the specific topic of spiritual disciplines, it really hits home with me. As followers of Christ, we must train, equip, and nurture our children so that they answer His call and enter into a relationship with Jesus Christ. However, we will only effectively develop in our children what *we* understand and know to be true.

Doug Lambert, lead pastor of Cincinnati Church of Christ, spoke forcefully in a sermon he gave the day our son was baptized in February 2014. He said that the most important thing we can do for our children is to "be well" spiritually. Doug also added that if activities and commitments are getting in the way of our families' health, then we need to back out of them now! Whatever *it* is, it's not more important than your spiritual health or your children's future.

Spiritual disciplines must be implemented in our lives in order to cultivate our relationship with God and help us to know Him better. These are the avenues whereby we grow in our faith and stay connected to Him. However big He is to you, that is how your children will view God. When we don't have our own relationship right with the Lord, how can we effectively lead our family toward Him? Developing closeness to God and enhancing our relationship with Him is crucial to the health of parents and their children.

I feel compelled to address the term *legalism* here. Thomas Constable states in his commentary, "Legalism is a human attitude by which we approach the standards set by God. It involves judging the behavior of ourselves, or others, as acceptable or unacceptable to God by the standard of obedience to laws that we, rather than God, have imposed."

I write this because, first of all, the spiritual disciplines I present to you are merely tools, not rules. Checking these off our to-do list does not bring us closer to God.

Second, the organized church today, with all of its denominational guidelines and traditions, in my opinion, sometimes misses the mark that God has authored. Teaching the Jesus of the Bible cannot be dismissed or overlooked in order to maintain our own belief systems and traditions. Always use the Bible as your primary source of information and inspiration!

There is an expectation within the Bible that followers of Jesus are to grow and mature in their faith. Paul uses the illustration of milk and solid food to make his point in Hebrews 5:12–14: "For though by this time you ought to be teachers, you need someone to teach you again the basic principles of the oracles of God. You need milk, not solid food, for everyone who lives on milk is unskilled in the word of righteousness, since he is a child. But solid food is for the mature, for those who have their powers of discernment trained by constant practice to distinguish good from evil."

So let's take a look at some ways in which we can grow in our relationship with Jesus.

Prayer

Prayer, or talking with God, is a necessary spiritual discipline. You may express your thoughts to God, and He will meet you there. Expect that you will be in His presence, and thank Him for who He is. Dedicate your life to Him, and then be quiet. Ask Him to speak to you, and jot down any responses He provides.

If you are at a loss for words, pray Scripture. Matthew 6:9–13 is commonly known as the Lord's Prayer. Jesus presented it to the disciples so they would have a model to follow. It contains petitions, three that relate more directly to God and three that relate to us. It reads like this:

"Our Father in heaven, hallowed be your name." (He is holy and deserves to be acknowledged that way.)

"Your kingdom come, your will be done on earth as it is in heaven." (God's kingdom is already present on earth, and doing His will should be our primary concern. Our prayer should be for Jesus to return soon, as we long for this.)

"Give us today our daily bread." (Meet our needs.)

"Forgive us our debts, as we also have forgiven our debtors." (Pardon our sins, and we will pardon others.)

"And lead us not into temptation, but deliver us from the evil one." (Do not let us succumb to Satan's trials and sin against You.)

When I am feeling down, or the world is crashing in around me, I focus on three verses that reveal God's truth. The first verse is John 16:33, where Jesus said, "In this world you will have tribulation, but take heart; I have overcome the world!" If we get comfortable and satisfied with how things are going in our lives, then trouble may not be clearly evident to us and our families. We may believe that God is blessing us and that we are living "right," but we must be careful. Satan is less likely to interfere in our lives when we are not doing anything to advance God's kingdom. When we are at war against the Enemy, things get messy!

Romans 8:28 speaks to me also. "And we *know* that for those who love God *all* things work together for good, for those who are called according to his purpose." I emphasize "know" and "all," because it's not just a "maybe" that God is in our lives and orchestrating everything that occurs. We can be certain and trust that He is present. Once again, though, this is not to say that we will always feel good or be comfortable with a circumstance. It is to say that God has our lives in His hands and that we can rest assured that He will always have our best interests in mind.

Finally, I often remember Philippians 4:13: "I can do everything (all things!) through Christ who gives me strength." My daughter Abby has a tattoo with this verse, and I remember my kids singing a song with these lyrics when they were little children. This is an important verse, but it may be misunderstood by some. We can do anything, as long as it is within God's will for us.

Knowing the teachings of Christ makes it possible for us to pray effectively. Find the verses that speak to you, and keep them at the forefront of your mind.

Prayer was a dominant discipline in Jesus' life and a recurring part of His teaching. The book of Luke gives many examples of Jesus praying alone, in small groups and in front of large masses. He often retreated to pray alone, and in Luke 6, He spent the night on a mountainside before selecting the twelve disciples. Jesus took

Peter, James, and John with him to pray on a mountaintop. As He prayed, "the appearance of his face changed, and his clothes became as bright as a flash of lightning" (Luke 9:28–29). Even as He was dying on the cross, Jesus prayed for those who were dividing up His clothes because, "they do not know what they are doing." Prayer was a necessity for Jesus to stay connected to His Father, so it only makes sense that it is an important discipline for us too.

A simple acronym, ACTS, helped me learn to pray when I first became a follower of Jesus Christ.

- Adoration: God is the Lord of all the earth. He alone deserves our admiration and praise.
- Confession: We are imperfect people, and admitting our sins to Him sets us free. "If we confess our sins, he is faithful and just to forgive us our sins and to cleanse us from all unrighteousness" (1 John 1:9).
- Thanksgiving: "Pray without ceasing, give thanks in all circumstances; for this is the will of God in Christ Jesus for you" (1 Thessalonians 5:17–18).
- Supplication: We may lay our requests before the Creator of the universe, and He will hear us. "And this is the confidence that we have toward him, that if we ask anything according to his will he hears us" (1 John 5:14).

When parents pray, God will strengthen and enhance every aspect of their lives. Conversing with God leaves an impression on us, and throughout the day, awareness of Him remains. Please pray without ceasing, parents! Raising children will take us to our knees at times, and we must fight for them and ask God for His help. He alone is faithful and available to us at all times.

Reading the Bible

Studying Scripture prepares a parent for the challenges and predicaments that occur in all families. Knowing God's love and His promises to believers enables a Christian parent to grow and persevere through difficult times. The Word removes complacency and replenishes it with a life of learning, allowing leaders of their homes to face the next challenge or temptation coming down the road.

We are living in times that include the New Age movement, which is not really new. John, the son of Zebedee in the New Testament, addressed concerns about gnosticism to the early church. Gnosticism was heresy that was very dangerous to the first- and second-century church. Its central teaching was that spirit is entirely good and matter is completely evil. The book, 1 John, was written to expose false teachers and to give believers assurance of salvation through Jesus Christ. This was just the beginning of gnosticism, or the New Age movement. It has grown and grown over the ages, and our children are up against it, big-time.

New Age teachings focus on individual autonomy, relativism, and spiritualism. In the 1970s David Spangler believed that a release of new waves of spiritual energy, signaled by astrological changes, had initiated the coming of the new age. It united a body of diverse believers with two simple ideas.

First, it predicted that a new age of heightened spiritual consciousness and international peace would arrive and bring an end to racism, poverty, sickness, hunger, and war. This social transformation would result from the massive spiritual awakening of the general population during the next generation.

Second, individuals could obtain a foretaste of the new age through their own spiritual transformation. Initial changes would put the believer on the *sadhana*, a new path of continual growth and transformation. *Spirituality* is a common term used by Western culture. It involves a person's spirit and is concerned with an individual's religious values. Religion is observed and devotion is shown through supernatural beings and immaterial phenomena.

Tools that assist people in their personal transformation include astrology, yoga, meditation techniques, tarot readings, mediums, and the use of crystals. Spiritual groups such as guilds, societies, freemasonry, fraternities, and so on exist to provide like-minded believers opportunity to congregate and pass on the knowledge they possess.

I address this subject because you and your children are going to face this mind-set daily, perhaps without recognizing it. Maybe you are becoming aware of some the avenues of this thinking for the first time. I was in a class one day, and the idea was presented that "we create our own truth by simply believing it." How often have you heard someone say that reality and truth are what you make it?

Reading Scripture is vital to understanding and knowing the real truth. Parents must embrace this discipline wholeheartedly in order to mature and teach our children well, "so that we may no longer be children, tossed to and fro by the waves and carried about by every wind of doctrine, by human cunning, by craftiness in deceitful schemes" (Ephesians 4:14).

Solitude

Solitude is the discipline of spending time alone with God. This might last for five to ten minutes—or possibly hours. Parents might find this difficult to do, especially with little ones running around, but it is nonetheless crucial to our relationship with the Lord. You may have to wake up a few minutes early or go to bed a little later in order to make that connection. Whatever you must do, make it a priority to spend time alone with Him. Jesus modeled this regularly as an essential habit throughout His ministry.

Silence is a part of solitude where we are away from human contact, and all electronic devices are turned off. Today's world struggles mightily with this, in my opinion. Being alone for any length of time and being silent are too rare. When we sit still, take a walk, or jog, these can be times of silence—unless we choose to listen to an iPod or other type of listening device. That is not silence! Don't confuse silence with having the TV on for background noise or listening to the car radio with the volume turned down low. In order to focus on God, our environment must be quiet. I sit in our closet or bathroom to escape our dogs and extraneous noises. If necessary, I wear ear plugs.

Solitude gives parents space to change their innermost attitudes, which may relate to people around them or upcoming events. Listening to God takes the world off our shoulders for a time and interrupts our habit of constantly managing things and being in control (or thinking we are), and causes us to focus on Him alone. Fight against being too busy to develop this discipline. It is a major spiritual achievement to develop the capacity to do nothing in order to hear from God.

Accountability

An accountability relationship involves having a truth teller to keep us on track, a person with whom we can share our vulnerabilities.

Parents cannot always rely on their own perspectives of the way things are going. Typically, an accountability partner is a close friend or companion, not a spouse. Both partners are usually of the same sex, so vulnerabilities may be shared freely. It is a reciprocal relationship, and both people must be willing to be open and honest.

An accountability partner also provides encouragement and feedback. All parents do the best they can, but they still need outside information to help them see how they are doing. What seems like a problem that cannot be overcome may be an issue another parent is going through as well. Amazingly, when you hear friends telling stories similar to your own, the situation becomes a little less daunting.

Another reason to find a confidant is that the person holding you accountable will speak truth into your life. Truth tellers are important and probably furnish you with the greatest opportunity for growth. Growth and maturity take place in two ways: first, feedback is welcomed, and second, vulnerabilities are shared.

Feedback is a gift. When a person is willing to accept feedback, the partner providing the feedback is appreciated, not dismissed. Sometimes what a person has to say may be difficult to hear. Parents who are unwilling to listen to feedback get blindsided, even though people were available to give helpful information.

Sharing and being vulnerable expose issues inside of us that we may need to release to God and repent of. We must be willing to open ourselves up and be honest with an accountability partner. Choose carefully this friend that you allow into your innermost feelings and thoughts. Proverbs 18:24 reminds us, "A man of many companions may come to ruin, but there is a friend who sticks closer than a brother." Not everyone can fill this role for you. If you do not have a special person like this in your life at this time, pray and ask God to bring one to you.

Accountability may be uncomfortable, but it is necessary. It is a two-way street between true friends who bear each other's burdens and rejoice in one another's successes. Ecclesiastes 4:12 states, "And though a man might prevail against one who is alone, two will withstand him—a threefold cord is not quickly broken." We all need other people in our lives to speak truth to us in love.

Generous Giving

Did you know that Jesus addressed the topic of money in approximately 20 to 25 percent of His teachings? The New Testament is loaded with wisdom when it comes to our money and possessions. When Jesus came to the earth, He gave His whole life and fulfilled the old covenant of tithing. Then the new mandate of giving generously was introduced. Giving back to God is a spiritual discipline that deserves attention, especially in light of the materialism and wealth we experience today.

Matthew 6:21 and Luke 12:34 both say, "For where your treasure is, there your heart will be also." What does it mean to lay up treasures in heaven? It means to use all that we have for the glory of God. We are to let go when it comes to the material things of life. Believers measure life by the true riches of the kingdom and not by the false riches of this world.

Everything we have has been given to us by God. When we give generously, God blesses us in proportion to the amount by which we bless others. This does not mean that God will "prosper" us or give us more. What it does mean is that He will provide us with more opportunities to help more people. Also, as we give, He will increase our desire to give.

Having money is not a bad thing, but 1 Timothy 6:10 tells us that "the love of money is the root of all evil." Do you hate to part with your money? Or do you save so much for a rainy day that you are afraid to give it away? Generous giving should not be done grudgingly.

Consider these three areas when you determine how you will give generously. First, give to your local church, as they are your family. Second, outside agencies or parachurch organizations that focus on international missions can be worthwhile avenues for you to support. And third, keep a small account for the unexpected needs of others. Helping those around us in their time of need is essential to giving.

Advancing God's kingdom and bringing Him praise and glory should be our motivation to give. It is a matter of the heart. Only you and God know the motives and reasoning behind your giving. Pray that God will show you how and where to generously give so that *He* is your treasure, not the world and its possessions.

Other Disciplines

There are many more spiritual disciplines to consider that create inward growth and change. Without going into much detail, I want to present a few others.

Serving, not only with your family, can also be considered a spiritual discipline that God calls us to do. Galatians 5:13–14 says, "For you were called to freedom, brothers. Only do not use your freedom as an opportunity for the flesh, but through love serve one another. For the whole law is fulfilled in one command: 'You shall love your neighbor as yourself.'" Jesus, the Son of God, served with humility and selflessness, and ultimately He sacrificed His own life for us. Mark 10:45 and Mathew 20:28 say, "For even the Son of Man came not to be served but to serve, and to give his life as a ransom for many." Shouldn't we follow His lead?

Spending time with the body of Christ is another spiritual discipline. Hopefully, you have a local church body near you that is mission-minded and family-friendly. Churches must be led by humble, godly servants who understand that all areas under their leadership must point to Jesus alone. These leaders must also assist parents with the teaching and equipping of their children, rather than assuming the lead. Mom and Dad continue to be the most influential people in their children's lives. How does the church you attend teach and equip you?

Fasting is a spiritual discipline that occurs throughout the Bible. To fast is to abstain from food over a period of time. It is a time between God and you, and it is not meant for others to know about. Matthew 6:16–18 says, "And when you fast, do not look gloomy like the hypocrites, for they disfigure their faces that their fasting may be seen by others. Truly, I say to you, they have received their reward. But when you fast, anoint your head and wash your face, that your fasting may not be seen by others but by your Father who is in secret. And your Father who sees in secret will reward you."

God is faithful and will take the lead as you examine the spiritual disciplines in your life. To excel in anything, discipline is required. This is true for athletes, musicians, plumbers, accountants, and disciples of Jesus. Disciplines don't set aside our need for grace; nor do they earn us anything. They are simply a means to help us be with Jesus and become like Him.

9

No Greater Love

"'And you shall love the Lord your God with all your heart and with all your soul and with all your mind and with all your strength.' The second is this: 'You shall love your neighbor as yourself.' There is no other commandment greater than these" (Mark 12:30–31).

Jesus spoke these words, and we call them the Great Commandment. It is crucial that we digest this mandate in the proper order. We are to love God first and love others second, which includes our children, spouse, family members, friends, and so on.

This story is about a couple who understood that no matter what happened, God was sovereign and their first love. No circumstance or lack of understanding of who He is deterred them from praising, trusting, and loving Him, first and foremost, through very trying months. Amy and Jeremiah's faith has touched many people, and I pray that when parenting gets hard, you will remember this: God loves you and your children more than you can ever think or imagine!

Living Grace: a blog by Amy Whitsel, February 2014

Brody Micah Whitsel has changed our lives. He was diagnosed with anencephaly at twenty weeks' gestation. Learning that he wouldn't live past birth was devastating. As we have chosen to carry him to term, and he is due in February 2014, I've learned a lot, and I've learned that I love to write. Hopefully, my feeble words and grammatical errors will contain words of hope, inspiration, and comfort for all who suffer. May it all point to the one who offers us life through His grace.

Brody, the days and weeks that followed your diagnosis were flooded with moments of despair, anger, and confusion—and moments of peace, hope, and trust in our God. The prayers of so many people were probably the only thing that kept me from letting go of that thin thread of life. My dear husband, your daddy, was and still is amazing. He constantly reminded me of God's promises and the fact that He had us—and you, our dear son—in His hands.

We quickly decided on your name: Brody Micah Whitsel. Jeremiah had thought of the name Brody before we were even pregnant, and Micah randomly popped into my head during the ultrasound before the devastating news. We learned that Micah means "Who is like our God?," and Brody comes from a Gaelic name that means "ditch." *Oh no!* I thought. *Can we still use it?* But Miah was quick to point out that when we are in life's ditch, who is like our God?

Brody, I can't tell you how much I enjoyed carrying you to term! On some days, it felt like you would never come, as I couldn't wait to see you and hold you. On other days, it felt like each moment of each day was slipping away too fast, as I cried in anticipation of having to let you go. We were determined to be obedient to God and not end your life earlier than He intended. In our last month with you, I cried most nights as your daddy and I went to bed. But he just kept saying, "We get to hold him! We get to see him soon!" We clung to this hope and also to the fact that you would soon get to be in Jesus' arms.

When you finally came, I knew immediately that your delivery had put too much stress on you, and that you were already safe in Jesus' arms. I didn't mind. I just wanted to hold you and take in every inch of your perfect body.

The flurry of nurses and everyone around us disappeared as I took you in my arms. Voices sounded distant, and my pain seemed irrelevant. Your daddy and I stared at you and took your tiny hands in ours. I can't explain the love and joy I felt. You were here! And you were ours. How could God be so gracious and loving to grant us this gift?

The hours that followed, so very early on that Monday morning, were precious. Your daddy and I were surprised by how quickly we wanted our family to come in and meet you! I was so sad that you were so bruised, but Miah kept saying, "He's perfect!" And I couldn't have agreed more.

My dear Brody, I could go on and on about our sweet moments with you and about how very happy I, your mommy, and Miah, your daddy, are to call you our son. As I've contemplated this journey and all the details surrounding your birth, I've certainly had my questions. I asked God why your birth had to be so physically painful after all we'd been through. Why did your precious little body have to be so bruised? Why couldn't He have given you to us alive, even if only for a few minutes?

God, in His loving graciousness, gave me some answers. It was your daddy who first said that perhaps it was God's grace to us that you were stillborn. Maybe it would've been too hard to see you breathe and move—and then have to watch you pass. When you were handed to us, you were already at perfect peace, free from pain and in the presence of our Lord! Later, when I thought of the pain, I was grateful.

Most moms look forward to a lifetime of giving everything they can for their children. This was my only chance with you. I would've suffered a million times more for you because I love you. As for the bruising and trauma to your body, I'm not sure why it happened, but I know this: it reminds me of how fragile and temporary this life is. We were made for so much more than this life. God created us to spend a glorious eternity with Him!

My precious Brody Micah, I thank you for pointing us to God, for allowing us to marvel at His works, and for reminding us of the hope we have in Christ and His gift of eternity with Him (and you!) in heaven. Your daddy and I love you so very, very much, and we can't wait to see you again.

Love and kisses, with all our hearts,

Amy and Jeremiah, who will always be your mom and dad

10

A Very Brief History of Family Life throughout the Ages

The family unit is under great stress and scrutiny. Traditional families with a dad, a mom, and two kids (a boy and a girl) are no longer the typical, ideal scenario in the United States—and I would suggest that they really never have been. Looking back in history, the family unit has never been perfect, and parents and children have always struggled to some degree in their relationships with each other. When sin entered the world, all of our relationships took a hit.

Family dynamics have changed over the ages, but one thing has never changed, and that is our need for Creator God to be a part of it. Our hope is built on Jesus' blood and righteousness, and it is imperative that He be the center of our families. No matter what the circumstance of your family may be, Jesus is your strength and guide.

"Now to him who is able to do far more abundantly than all that we ask or think, according to the power at work within us, to him be glory in the church and in Christ Jesus throughout all generations, forever and ever. Amen" (Ephesians 3:20–21).

First Family

Adam and Eve were created by God in the beginning. They lived in a perfect situation and had full dominion over the earth, but they failed to follow God's instructions. Sin entered the world.

Adam and Eve had three sons: Cain, Abel, and later, Seth. Cain killed Abel when God accepted Abel's offering but not Cain's. Cain denied responsibility and was banished from God's presence, unable to enjoy his family's company. Cain was forced to wander from place to place, seeking food. This was the first dysfunctional family.

Ancient Rome in the First Century

Rome was a man's world. *Pater familias*, or the father of the family, was in charge. He was the oldest male, and everyone in the family obeyed him. His wife looked after the household, but he controlled it. He alone could own property, and only he could decide the fates of his children and whom they would marry. Children could be sold into slavery or killed. Sons were important to carry on the family name.

The Romans, however, expected a *pater familias* to treat his family fairly. There were no laws to stop him from treating them unfairly, but there was social pressure, especially when it came to respect and care for their elderly. When the older members of a family became too tired for other activities, they could always play with their grandchildren and great grandchildren, all of whom had been born under their roof. One day the family would honor them at the Parentalia, the festival of the dead.

Mothers who could read and write taught their children these skills. They also taught their girls how to cook, sew, and care for a family. Children were trained to obey their elders and to be loyal citizens. If a child talked back, he could find himself kicked out of his family's house forever. He could try to go to a friend's house, but the odds were good that the friend would not take him in. Basically, if a child was kicked out, it was likely that he would die soon.

The Middle Ages: The Fifth to Fifteenth Centuries

Children were generally miniatures of their parents, and they were expected to dress, talk, and act as adults. The only difference between adults and children was that the children had no rights. In some cases, children could be bought and sold by parents to make money. If the child was from a peasant home, he would be working in the fields or the kitchen as soon as possible. Middle-class children whose parents were artisans or merchants began to learn their parents' trade as soon as possible.

Very few people attended school in the Middle Ages. Most peasants learned their jobs and how to survive from their parents. Some children learned a craft through apprenticeship and the guild system. Wealthy children often learned through tutors. They would go to live in the castle of another lord, where they would work for the lord and learn about running a large manor.

A family unit included anyone living in the home, including servants, lodgers, or hired hands. Food, land, inheritance, reproduction, and education were all managed by the family.

The beginning of the Middle Ages is often called the Dark Ages. Very few people could read or write, and nobody expected conditions to improve. The only hope for most people during the Middle Ages was their strong Christian beliefs and the anticipation that life in heaven would be better than life on earth.

Renaissance or Early Modern Age: Fourteenth to Seventeenth Centuries

Men married in their twenties and women in their teens. The average life expectancy was forty, so families with grandparents were unusual. Still during the Renaissance, children were thought to be miniature adults. Therefore, as soon as they were out of diapers, they were dressed like adults and spoken to as adults.

Despite this grown-up treatment, children still had childhood toys and games to keep them occupied until they were deemed old enough to work at around age seven or eight. Toddlers were often confined to a wooden walker or tied to something with a long rope to prevent them from wandering off. This was important because a typical Renaissance house was full of burning fires and pots of boiling liquid.

Boys stayed home with their mothers until about the age of seven. Then they might go to a private school or be tutored, if the family could afford it. If not, boys were sent to work as a servant in a wealthy household. At age fourteen, boys could enter into an apprenticeship.

Girls, also, stayed home with their mothers, learning the necessary skills to run a household. If their family was poor, the girls might be put to work as domestic servants in wealthy households. A female was considered a "girl" until she married. If a woman never married, she was never considered fully grown. Wealthier girls received a limited education, focusing on history, Latin, geography, and the skills needed to be a good wife. Few women, though, received an education equal to that of males.

Elizabethan/Shakespearean Age: Sixteenth Century

Marriage in Elizabethan times appeared to be similar to marriages of today in that some of the traditions have remained constant. However, there were many key differences. For example, it was considered foolish to marry for love, and strangely enough, those who were of lower classes were more likely to have a choice in whom they married.

Everyone wanted (and expected) to have children. They were the property of their parents, and they were expected to give their parents the respect a servant gives his master—or else. Wives were the property of their husbands, and the previous expectations applied to them as well.

Every woman expected to be married and to depend on her male relatives throughout her life. Every man wanted to marry— or at least acknowledged that he must. If he was not noble, he had to marry in order to become the legal head of a household and to be eligible to hold public or ecclesiastical office and other positions of civic responsibility. If he became a widow, a man looked to remarry, especially if he had children. The traditional waiting period was called a "month's mind." To marry again after a month was not considered hasty.

The 1700s in Colonial America

Firmly established gender roles helped maintain strong family structures. The family was the basis for all other institutions. The government, church, and community all worked through the nuclear family unit.

As children, boys learned what it meant to be a man from the examples of their fathers. They also would have read the lengthy instructions for proper behavior in *The New England Primer*. Once they were apprenticed, boys were expected to learn and perform the duties of adult tradesmen.

By the age of thirteen, girls were expected to share in all the tasks of adult women. Women in colonial society were to maintain household order. They took care of young children, bought and prepared food, directed the activities of indentured servants or slaves, and performed all manner of other household chores. To encourage faith and moral development, mothers were often the primary spiritual instructors in the home, especially in the latter part of the seventeenth century.

A woman's identity and property were always connected with the men in her life. As a child, she was subordinate to her father. Upon marriage, she became a *feme covert*, and her identity and property then transferred to her husband.

Women living in the country were expected to do their productive work inside the home. This work was generally done for the benefit of the family and not the outside world. "Woman's work" would have included such activities as spinning, weaving, and churning. Mothers who could read also taught that skill to all their children.

The 1800s

By the end of the eighteenth century and into the nineteenth century, marriage was undertaken for affection, not for economic reasons. Courtship became more elaborate, and couples had more freedom. They attended dances, church socials, picnics, and concerts, and they got to know one another well. After the wedding, couples went on honeymoons to have a romantic interlude before settling down to daily life. Raising children became the most important job a wife performed, and children were to be loved and sheltered. Physical punishment of children did not disappear, but it became more moderate and was combined with encouragement and rewards.

The dominance of the family ideal is only one aspect of life in the nineteenth century. The constant emphasis on family, domesticity, and children could be confining, so men and women developed interests outside of the home. The nineteenth century was a great age of organizations for men only, and fraternal groups thrived. Taverns and barrooms provided a space for men to make political deals, secure jobs, and be entertained. Men formed literary and scientific societies, labor organizations, reform groups, Bible study groups, and sports leagues.

The nineteenth century was also a period of change for women. Married women who had more education and fewer children than their predecessors, founded reform groups, debating societies, and literary associations. They involved themselves in school reform, health issues, women's rights, temperance, child labor, and other public-policy issues. A few states in the West granted women full political rights. A women's movement demanding equal rights, including the vote, gained strength after 1848.

In the first half of the century, public education extended basic literacy to many poorer Americans, and in the second half of the century, women's high schools and colleges were founded, along with coeducational colleges in the Midwest and West. Women's occupational choices began to expand into the new fields of nursing, secretarial work, department store clerking, and more, although work was something a young woman did only until she married. Women who wanted a career had to forgo marriage.

By the middle of the nineteenth century, many states had passed laws allowing women control over their possessions and wages. A few states allowed divorce on the grounds of physical abuse. New stereotypes appeared at the same time. In child custody cases, women, rather than fathers, were given control of their children because women were considered natural child rearers. This practice would persist until the late twentieth century, when shared custody arrangements became common.

The Twentieth Century

Progressive Movement : 1890s–1920s

During this time, the government decided to implement social policies that created more nuclear families, the reason being was that it wanted to limit women in the workplace and outlaw child labor. Rising wages for male workers, the absence of union protection for women workers, and mandatory education laws allowed, or forced, more Americans to realize the domestic ideal. This occurred first in the North and then in the southern United States.

The Progressive Movement also brought about the modern social work movement. Trained social workers intervened in families experiencing problems that threatened the well-being of family members and affected the community: physical abuse, drug or alcohol addiction, neglect, or abandonment. Social workers were often successful in protecting the family, although social workers were sometimes influenced by the common prejudices of the time. Married women in the early twentieth century were discouraged from leaving abusive husbands because the prevailing belief was that a wife's place was in the home.

The Great Depression: 1930s

The Depression changed the family in dramatic ways. Many couples delayed marriage, and the divorce rate dropped sharply. (It was too expensive to pay the legal fees and support two households.) Birth rates dropped below the replacement level for the first time in American history. Families suffered a dramatic loss of income during Herbert Hoover's term in office. This put a great deal of stress on families. Some reacted by pulling together, making do with what they had, and turning to family and friends for help. Only after exhausting all alternatives would they reluctantly look to the government for help. Other families did not fare as well and ended up falling apart.

Traditional roles within the family changed during the 1930s. Men who found themselves out of work had to rely on their wives and children in some cases to help make ends meet. Many did not take this loss of power as the primary decision maker and breadwinner very well. Many stopped looking for work, paralyzed by their bleak chances and lack of self-respect. Some became so frustrated that they just walked out on their families completely. A 1940 survey revealed that 1.5 million married women had been abandoned by their husbands.

On the other hand, women found their status enhanced by their new roles. Left with little choice, they went against the historic opposition to married women working outside the home in order to help support their families. Black women especially found it easier to obtain work than their husbands did, and they worked as domestic servants, clerks, and textile workers, and in other occupations. This employment increased their status and power in the home, gaining them a new voice in domestic decisions.

World War II

During World War II, for the first time, large numbers of married women took jobs. Because of the war effort and the number of men sent overseas, women were hired to perform jobs traditionally done by men. The popular image of Rosie the Riveter captures the novelty of women dressed in work clothes, engaging in skilled, industrial labor. Factories set up day-care centers to attract married women workers. Women drove cabs, moved into positions with more responsibility, and provided support services for all the major branches of the armed forces. Although women earned lower wages, received fewer promotions, and were among the first to be laid off, the domestic image of women created in the late eighteenth and early nineteenth centuries had changed. Married women were out of the house and earning their own money.

The year after World War II ended, both the marriage rate and divorce rate soared. While divorce was not uncommon before the war, most divorces were sought by recently married couples without children or by older couples with grown children. Once children arrived, couples felt obliged to stay together for the sake of the children, no matter how uncomfortable or violent the marriage. Increasingly after World War II, and especially by the 1960s, the presence of children did not hinder divorce. Parents came to believe that it was better to rear children in a less stressful setting than to maintain the friction of marital success. Child custody became a divisive issue in divorces, adversely affecting parents and children.

The end of the war also rapidly reduced the number of married women employed outside the home, as returning veterans sought work. Many of these women gradually returned to work, either because they had enjoyed working, or because the family wanted the second income to buy a new home in the suburbs, a second automobile, a new television set, or other consumer goods that were now available. Some veterans took advantage of their military benefits to attend college while their wives worked.

A youth culture developed during and after World War II. High school students embraced fashions separate from their parents, new forms of music and dance, slang expressions, and sometimes freer attitudes toward sexuality, smoking, or drug use, which created a generation gap between parents and children. Still, parents were anxious to provide their children with advantages that had not existed during the depression and war years.

The Fifties and Sixties

Known as the "last age of innocence," the fifties were a time of buying binges and cheap houses, cars, and electronics. Families sat together for dinners, and a sense of harmony and peace existed within the home. Mom was home to look after the kids, and she supervised the homework and chores when the children got home from school. If a child was ever disrespectful to an adult, he or she was grounded or severely punished. There was a zero-tolerance policy for misbehaving.

Generally, it was safe to walk around at night, and parents worried less about their children's safety. If a child needed money for any desired items, girls babysat and boys flipped burgers or worked at a gas station to earn the money themselves.

More boys went to college than girls, who typically lived at home until they married. There were no "living together" arrangements in relationships. Women who did go to college were limited to careers as teachers, nurses, secretaries, stewardesses, and the like.

TV was not common, and people might watch a couple of hours if they were lucky. Because there were no computers, kids used their imaginations while playing outdoors with friends in the neighborhood. Hanging out with friends continued well into the teen years, and for the most part, kids got along well in groups, and there was less peer pressure. Clothing labels were unimportant, even though fashion mattered.

The Seventies and Eighties

By the 1970s approximately 61 percent of all married women were working outside the home, at least part-time. Women no longer felt as though they must get married because they were able to support themselves. Being single was now an acceptable alternative to being married. Society as a whole was more open-minded to a variety of living arrangements, family configurations, and lifestyles. "Free love," the development of new, effective contraceptives, and the legalization of abortion were evident in this new sexual revolution.

Expectations were high for marriages, and if they were not met, an unhappy spouse left. Life expectancies were longer, so grandparents were around to be a part of the children's lives. There was a sharp rise in yuppies, or young urban professionals, and making lots of money was associated with a good life. Attaining higher education was one way to become affluent.

The self-centered "me" generation was off and running. Interestingly, though, children left home later and approximately 40 percent returned for a time. This is referred to as the "boomerang effect." Awareness of AIDS became an issue that the world would have to deal with. This deadly disease could be spread through drugs and sex, so the "free love" expansion was somewhat scary as kids entered adulthood.

The 1990s: End of a Tumultuous Era

The divorce rate in the United States was the highest in the world, even though it appeared to be on a gradual decline. Educated women were having fewer children, but this allowed them to spend more time with each child. Fathers in the home were also spending more time with the children than ever before. Because people were living longer, couples had more time together as well. Parents shared the responsibilities of rearing children, and this was good for the kids. Yet childcare outside the home was at an all-time high.

Families no longer established or identified a line between "wants versus needs." Many couples were living beyond their means, and debt rose sharply. There was a growing use of computers, pagers, and cell phones, so communication expanded. Parents could now work from anywhere at any time. Women, particularly mothers, continued to flood the workforce.

Even with the threat of AIDS, the number of sexually active teens was significantly higher than in the previous ten years or so. Life in the 1990s was stressful to young people. As the percentage of the teenage population decreased relative to the adult world, the numbers of teenage pregnancies continued to rise. A growing number of minorities lived at the poverty level, and the number of single-parent households increased.

The Twenty-First Century

Two parents in the work force, delayed marriage, and a slight decline in the divorce rate were evident at the outset of the twenty-first century. The rapid growth of couples living together has slowed, and most will still get married eventually. A growing proportion of children have been born outside of marriage.

The high cost of education has caused college-age kids to stay home longer.

Problems of high and idealistic expectations for marriage, sexual relationships, and the parent/child relationship are causing more overt problems. Schools now need to provide social workers and psychologists, along with counselors, to address issues at home. Families are looking for perfection, but many are not willing to work at it, so tenuous relations are built. Many will experiment until they find a satisfying life for themselves.

Today

You are reading this now, and it is up to you to write your own family history. Parents always have been, and continue to be, the most influential people in the lives of their children. I hope that as you have read this, the Bible has inspired you to take your parenting to the next level.

God may have put one or more children into your life. Children are unaware of the dangers surrounding them in this world, and parents *must* be the ones who direct and guide their steps. Life is a series of choices, and my heart's desire is that this book will assist you as you raise your children. I hope it convicts you to the core that this is the most important "job" you will ever hold.

Your family's history starts and ends with you!

Sources

Anderson, Neil T. *Victory Over the Darkness*. Ventura: Regal Books, 1990.

Barna, George. *Transforming Children into Spiritual Champions*. Ventura: Regal Books, 2003.

Beck, Glenn. "Fighting against the Growing Entitlement Society." January 16, 2013. http://www.glennbeck.com/.

Constable, Thomas. "Expository Notes." 2014. *Sonic Light*. http://www.soniclight.com/.

Dobson, James. *The New Dare to Discipline*. Wheaton: Tyndale House Publishers, Inc., 1992.

Gray, Madison. "The Affluenza Defense: Judge Rules Rich Kid's Rich Kid-ness Makes Him Not Liable for Deadly Drunk Driving Accident." December 12, 2013. http://www.newsfeed.time.com.

MVParents of the Search Institute. "Community Involvement." January 20, 2006. http://www.mvparents.com.

Olive Tree Bible App. English Standard Version. 2014.

Piper, John. *Don't Waste Your Life*. Wheaton: Crossway Books, 2003.

Saban, Nick. *How Good Do You Want to Be?* New York: Ballantine Books, 2005.

Stanley, Andy. *Guardrails*. DVD. Grand Rapids: Zondervan, 2011.

Stearns, Peter. *Anxious Parents: A History of Modern Child-Rearing in America*. New York: New York University Press, 2002.

Taylor, Jim, PhD. "Is Technology Creating a Family Divide?" 2013. *Psychology Today*. http://www.psychologytoday.com

Whitsel, Amy. "To My Sweet Brody: A Summary of our Story." February 25, 2014. *Living Grace* blog. http://www. BrodyMicah.Blogspot.com.

The Years Fly by … But the Days Last Forever! brings insight to parenting through the most influential and important book of all times: the Bible.

Daily assertions and comments are made regarding the state of our children today along with the disarray of the family unit, but hope should not be lost! Difficulties and struggles within the family unit are not recent developments—it's just that now there is a greater number of people and more ways to hear about those problems.

James 4:14 asks, "What is your life? You are a mist that appears for a little while and then vanishes." Choosing to raise your children in a manner that honors God is your responsibility, but this opportunity is fleeting and vitally important.

The Years Fly by … But the Days Last Forever! addresses such areas as:

- Discipline
- Communication
- Being a role model
- Entitlement
- Who we are in Christ

All children are a gift from God. They are innocent, adaptable, and deserve to be taken care of. The world is vying for their attention, but parents must be the ones who direct and guide their steps. Life is full of choices. I hope that reading this will assist you as you raise your children and convince you to the core that this is the most important "job" you will ever hold!

Cathy Durrenberg comes from a long line of educators. She has worked as a teacher, an administrator, an adjunct professor, a school aide for multi handicapped students, and, in her most difficult job, a Mom.

In 2007, while completing her master's degree from the Alliance Theological Seminary, Cathy was inspired by God to work with families—primarily with parents. Her mission is to empower and equip them to be the spiritual leaders of their homes. Cathy currently lives in Kettering, Ohio, with her husband, Jon. She has three adult children.

WESTBOW·
PRESS
A DIVISION OF THOMAS NELSON
& ZONDERVAN